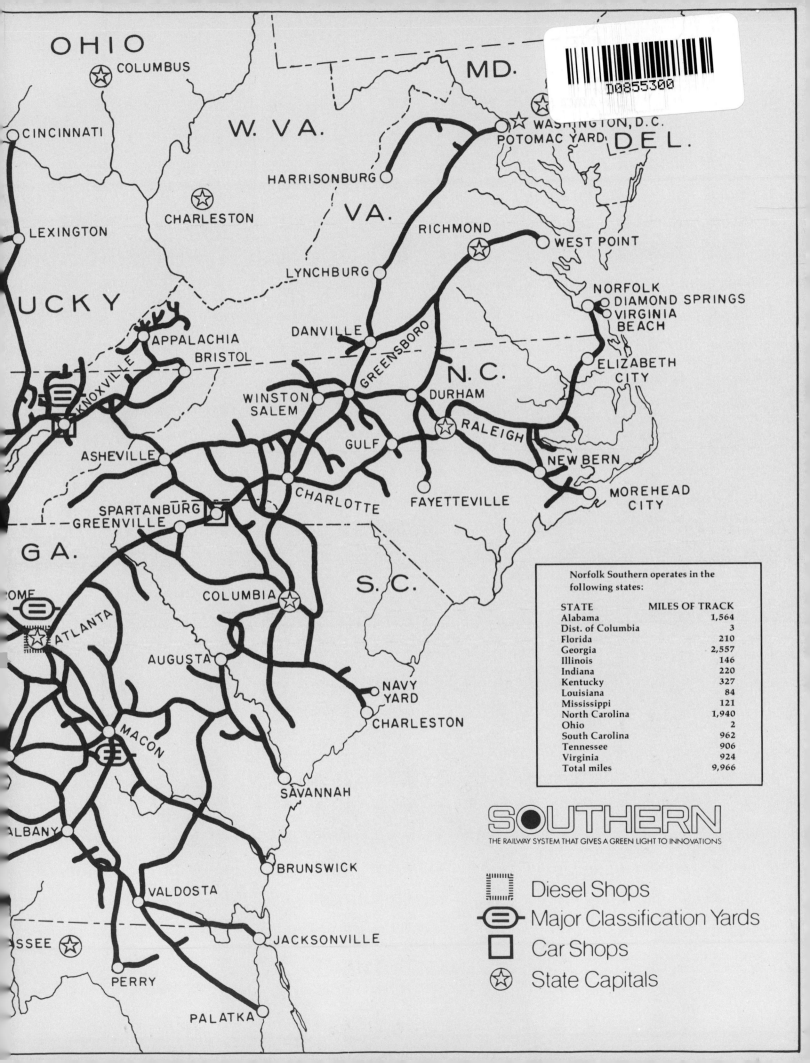

OHIO

COLUMBUS

W. VA.

MD.

CINCINNATI

HARRISONBURG

CHARLESTON

VA.

LEXINGTON

RICHMOND

WASHINGTON, D.C.
POTOMAC YARD

DEL.

WEST POINT

LYNCHBURG

NORFOLK
DIAMOND SPRINGS
VIRGINIA
BEACH

UCKY

APPALACHIA

DANVILLE

GREENSBORO

N.C.

ELIZABETH
CITY

BRISTOL

KNOXVILLE

WINSTON
SALEM

DURHAM

ASHEVILLE

GULF

RALEIGH

NEW BERN

CHARLOTTE

FAYETTEVILLE

MOREHEAD
CITY

SPARTANBURG
GREENVILLE

GA.

COLUMBIA

S. C.

OME

ATLANTA

AUGUSTA

NAVY
YARD

CHARLESTON

MACON

SAVANNAH

ALBANY

BRUNSWICK

VALDOSTA

SSEE

JACKSONVILLE

PERRY

PALATKA

Norfolk Southern operates in the following states:	
STATE	MILES OF TRACK
Alabama	1,564
Dist. of Columbia	3
Florida	210
Georgia	2,557
Illinois	146
Indiana	220
Kentucky	327
Louisiana	84
Mississippi	121
North Carolina	1,940
Ohio	2
South Carolina	962
Tennessee	906
Virginia	924
Total miles	9,966

SOUTHERN
THE RAILWAY SYSTEM THAT GIVES A GREEN LIGHT TO INNOVATIONS

Diesel Shops

Major Classification Yards

Car Shops

State Capitals

THE
SOUTHERN RAILWAY
SYSTEM
AN ILLUSTRATED HISTORY

Inman Yards, 1949.

– Fred W. Bruce.

THE
SOUTHERN
RAILWAY
SYSTEM

AN ILLUSTRATED HISTORY

SOUTHERN RAILWAY
SERVES THE SOUTH
SR
LOOK AHEAD - LOOK SOUTH

by
William Webb

THE BOSTON MILLS PRESS

This run-through train is southbound from Columbus, Ohio, via Cincinnati as it crosses the Emory River near Nemo, Tenn., in 1970.
— *Norfolk Southern Corp.*

Acknowledgements

I hereby give full credit to the Southern Railway System for the material used in writing this book. All material and photos, unless otherwise marked, are from Southern Railway files.

I wish to thank Mrs. Marci Larson for her help and cooperation in the writing of this book. Also I wish to thank some very special friends for their help.

Mr. Walter Johnson	*Mr. Bill Gibson*
Mr. Bob Jones	*Mr. John A. Smith*
Mr. C.E. Head	*Mr. Frank M. Kaylor*
Mr. Eugene S. Eanes	*Mr. Edward E. Mickens*
Mr. G. Howard Gregory	*Mr. Frank E. Ardrey, Jr.*

Maintenance Section TM35

W.W.

Cataloguing in Publication Data

Webb, William.
 The story of the Southern Railway System

ISBN 0-919783-19-8

1. Southern Railway (U.S.) - History.
I. Title.

TF25.S7W42 1986   385'.09755   C86-093443-8

Published by:
THE BOSTON MILLS PRESS
132 Main Street
Erin, Ontario N0B 1T0, Canada
(519) 833-2407

American Association
for State and Local History
Award of Merit

Winners of the
Heritage Canada
Communications Award

Design by John Denison
Cover Photo – Norfolk Southern Corp.
Typeset by Lexigraf, Tottenham
Printed by Ampersand, Guelph

Cover Photo – A Northbound run-through train crossing the Cumberland River in Kentucky; typifies Norfolk Southern single-system service.

– Norfolk Southern Corp.

Dedicated to the Memory of my Beloved Sister
Mrs. Geraldine Amanda Webb Brown
1937 — 1979

Preface

The Southern Railway began operations in 1894, although the lines that would make up this system date back to 1827. A little six-mile line in South Carolina was the beginning of a system that today operates 9,966 miles of track in 13 states.

This story begins with the South Carolina Canal & Rail Road Company in 1827, and traces the histories of the other companies that 67 years later would be important links in a much greater system.

These early lines were not without their share of construction problems, but the biggest problem was the Civil War; these early lines went to war in 1861 and were in it until the end. After the war, there were a few railroads that were able to start operations, but for others the only way to survive was to merge with their stronger neighbors.

In 1894, the Southern Railway started operations, and this work traces the important things that have happened from that time until the merger between Southern and Norfolk & Western in 1982.

The Southern Railway helped to shape the South of yesterday and today, and will continue to shape the South of tomorrow.

Southern No. 2187, GP-7 single unit on local freight on Hendersonville-Lake Toxaway line, 1953.
- Photo by R.D. Sharpless, collection of F.E. Ardrey, Jr.

Contents

I   9

The Early Lines
1827 – 1859

II   21

The War Years
1860 – 1865

III   35

Reconstruction
1866 – 1870

IV   41

Transition
1871 – 1893

V   47

Southern Railway
1894 – 1982

Here Southern No. 949 wears green
and gold as she sits on the turntable at
Selma, Ala., 1947.

– Photo by F.E. Ardrey, Jr.

Southern Railway's 1928 replica of the *Best Friend of Charleston*. The original locomotive began operating on December 25, 1830, and was the first locomotive built in America for regular railroad service.

– *Norfolk Southern Corp.*

Chapter I

The Early Lines
1827 – 1859

Lines that were to become part of the Southern Railway System played an important part in the railroad development of the South, so much so that to follow their growth it is necessary to go back to the very beginnings of railroads in this country.

The opening of the Erie Canal in November 1825 is generally considered to have given the spur to American enterprise in the construction of artificial highways. Until that time rivers had borne most of the country's commerce, and in that respect the South was better favored than any other section of the country. Surrounded by navigable waters and intersected by a network of navigable streams, the agricultural South had seen her cities spring up on the banks or at the mouths of her rivers, where they could best serve their function of collecting and transporting agricultural products and distributing imported merchandise.

At first, cities developed according to the commerce along their rivers. By 1825, however, many of the older cities of the Seaboard, such as Charleston, Savannah, Richmond, Norfolk, Petersburg and Wilmington, were beginning to reach out in commercial rivalry for new sources of supply and new markets for distribution. They were ready to take to heart the lesson of the Erie Canal.

Virginia's pioneering work of internal improvement, the James River and Kanawha Canal, was hardly under way before the success of Stephenson's locomotive at the Rainhill trials in England in 1828 focused the world's attention on construction of railroads.

From then until 1836, most of the states of the South began work on more railroad lines to serve local needs and aid in the development of their respective cities. Most of these early lines were designed to reach some navigable river within or near the borders of a single state. Until 1836, the daring suggestion of great trunk lines across several states was not entertained in the South.

The early railroads of the South which were opened or well under construction by 1836 may be classified into four general groups: (1) the South Carolina group, (2) the Virginia group, (3) the Tennessee River group, and (4) the Georgia group. All but the fourth contained lines that later became part of the Southern Railway System.

It was on the South Carolina Canal & Rail Road Company track, on December 25, 1830, that a steam locomotive began regular service for the first time on this continent. The event occurred in Charleston, S.C., and marked the real beginning of steam railroads in this country.

The locomotive was the famous *Best Friend of Charleston*, a name given to it by businessmen who saw in the railroad a means of preserving Charleston as a great seaport, by providing good transportation at low cost between the port and the fast-developing inland areas.

Chartered in December 1827, construction of the road was begun in January 1830. By the end of 1830, only six miles of road had been completed, making the *Best Friend*'s first run necessarily short. However, on October 1, 1833, the railroad was opened for its entire 136-mile length, from Charleston to Hamburg, S.C. At the time it was the longest railroad in the world, and it had already become, in 1831, the first railroad to carry the United States Mail.

As crowds approached the appointed spot to witness the departure of the first scheduled steam locomotive, they saw a small locomotive attached to two high-side wooden wagons with bare board benches for seats. Smoke swirled from the bottle-shaped boiler and smokestack, steam hissed into the inclined cylinders, pistons began to move and the iron-tired wheels began to turn on this historic trip. Passengers cheered as the *Best Friend* headed down the track, and they gripped the sides of the cars as the locomotive gathered speed.

Away they flew, as one passenger described it, "on wings of the wind at the speed of 15 to 25 miles an hour, annihilating time and space and leaving all the world behind." Returning from the intersection of State and Dorchester roads (as far as the roadbed was then completed), the engine "darted forth like a live rocket, scattering sparks and flames on either side, passing over three saltwater creeks, hop, step and jump, and landed us all safe at the lines before any of us had the time to determine whether or not it was prudent to be scared."

What manner of engine was this *Best Friend* that made such a hit with Charleston passengers? Physically, it was a lightweight in comparison to the powerful locomotives we know today. It tipped the scales at less than five tons and developed only 6 to 12 horsepower, with a speed, running light, of 30 miles an hour, of 20 miles an hour when hauling a train of cars. All four wheels were driving wheels and worked on a double crank from two inclined cylinders mounted inside the locomotive frame at the front end. Connecting rods joined the two wheels at each side. At the rear of the locomotive, a bottle-shaped metal chimney enclosed a vertical boiler with a furnace at the bottom and outlets leading to the outer jacket and smokestack. Built at the West Point Foundry in New York City at a cost of $4,000, the engine was ordered and paid for by one of the directors, E.L. Miller, a Charleston merchant, after a smaller model steam locomotive had worked successfully. It arrived in the city aboard the boat *Niagara* on October 23, 1830. After it was assembled and tested in trial runs in early December, the railway purchased the locomotive from Miller.

In the early stages of the road's planning, the directors had debated at some length whether to use horse-drawn cars or steam locomotives. Miller and Horatio Allen, the road's chief engineer, strongly favored the locomotive.

"But the basis of the official act" (the board's decision to adopt the steam locomotive), as Allen wrote later, "was . . . on the broad ground that in the future there was no reason to expect any material improvement in the breed of horses, while in my judgement, the man was not living who knew what the breed of locomotives was to place at command . . ."

Before the decision to use steam power was reached, the South Carolina Canal & Rail Road Company encouraged numerous experiments with motive power. A sail car, rigged to a small boat and powered by the wind, figured in one of the early experiments, but never amounted to more than an interesting novelty.

More serious attention centered around cars moved by horsepower or manpower. Several of these raced in time trials in September 1830 for the $300 in prizes offered by the railroad to stimulate interest in designing such cars. The winning vehicle, a car powered by a horse walking a treadmill geared to the wheels, outstripped two similar cars using men in shifts of two. Completed and tested on the road, *The Flying Dutchman*, as the car was called, carried 12 passengers at a speed of 12 miles an hour.

But with the arrival of the *Best Friend* and the successful Christmas debut, other forms of motive power faded into the background. Steam had won first place, and the pressing problems were the completion of the road and the purchase of more engines and cars.

A second locomotive, *The West Point*, was ordered from the West Point Foundry by Horatio Allen, who had sent plans and drawings. Completed and delivered to Charleston by boat in February 1831, the new engine was the same size as the *Best Friend* but had a horizontal tubular boiler. The *West Point* went into service on a regular basis in July 1831 (it wasn't satisfactory in early trials). It was the road's only engine in service until February 1832, when the *South Carolina* arrived. Other locomotives were added in the next three years.

The *Best Friend* came to grief just six months after its first run. A sensitive fireman, annoyed by the hissing steam escaping from the boiler safety valve, proceeded to hold down the valve. The resulting explosion blew the fireman to kingdom come and the locomotive into a fine assortment of pieces. But the thrifty railroad used the running parts of the *Best Friend* to build another locomotive, *The Phoenix*.

Two months after charter of the South Carolina Canal & Rail Road Company, a railroad known as the Chesterfield Railroad Company was chartered in Virginia in February 1828. It built and operated a ten-mile line, from the coal fields of Chesterfield County to the tidewater of the James River opposite Richmond. (In 1851, the Richmond & Danville Railroad Company completed a parallel line that ended the history of the Chesterfield Railroad, and seven years afterward bought the property outright.) The other early railroads in the Virginia group did not become part of the Southern.

In Alabama, a charter was obtained for the Tuscumbia Railway Company in January 1830 and construction began on a railroad from the town of Tuscumbia to the Tennessee River. This two-mile line was opened in 1932 and operated so successfully that a charter was immediately obtained for the Tuscumbia, Courtland & Decatur Railroad Company to extend the railroad along the valley of the Tennessee River 43 miles to Decatur.

It was expected that the line would carry the through-river traffic at that time interrupted by Muscle Shoals. The line was opened in 1834. A year later an attempt was made by the La Grange & Memphis Railroad Company to open a line from La Grange, Tennessee, to the Mississippi River at Memphis, with the expectation that it could later be extended to a connection with the Tuscumbia, Courtland & Decatur. However, after six miles of road were constructed out of Memphis, the line was temporarily abandoned in 1837.

The growth of trade between the South and the fast-developing area that now includes Ohio, Indiana and Illinois — then known as "the West" — went forward in the first quarter of the nineteenth century despite the mountain barriers which made overland travel difficult and which sent much of the commerce by the more cir-cuitous route down the Ohio and Mississippi rivers to New Orleans, from there by ship to the ports of the Atlantic Seaboard and up the rivers to the interior.

When the people of Charleston, S.C., saw their first railroad enterprise brought to successful completion in 1833, they were emboldened to undertake an even greater project, a through line from Charleston to the Ohio River. The Louisville, Cincinnati & Charleston Railroad Company (LC&C) was chartered, and commissioners were sent to interest the states of North Carolina, Tennessee and Kentucky in this enterprise.

Horatio Allen (1802–1890), Chief Engineer of the South Carolina Canal and Rail Road Co. from 1829-35.
– *Norfolk Southern Corp.*

At the famous "Knoxville Convention" in July 1836, delegates from all the interested states heard resolutions adopted to construct — using charters already granted to the LC&C by several states — a railroad from Charleston via Columbia, S.C., Asheville, N.C., the valley of the French Broad River, Paint Rock, N.C., and then into Tennessee, passing through Knoxville, north to Lexington, Kentucky, with three lines branching from there to Louisville, Cincinnati and Maysville. Branches into Georgia and Virginia from the main line were also contemplated in the work, which was estimated to cost $12 million.

Financial panic in 1837 effectively doomed the enterprise. The line from Branchville to Columbia, built by the South Carolina road, was the only tangible result. (The South Carolina company later became the South Carolina Railroad. It struggled through war, rebuilding and later bankruptcy before becoming part of the Southern Railway in 1899.) It is interesting to note, however, that the Southern now operates a line between Charleston and Louisville and Cincinnati, almost exactly the same as the one envisioned by this convention.

On December 20, 1833, a charter was granted by the state legislature of Georgia to the Central Rail Road & Canal Company for the purpose of laying, building and making railroad and canal communications from the City of Savannah to the interior of the state. Subsequently, the charter was amended and the name of the company was changed to the Central Rail Road & Banking Company of Georgia.

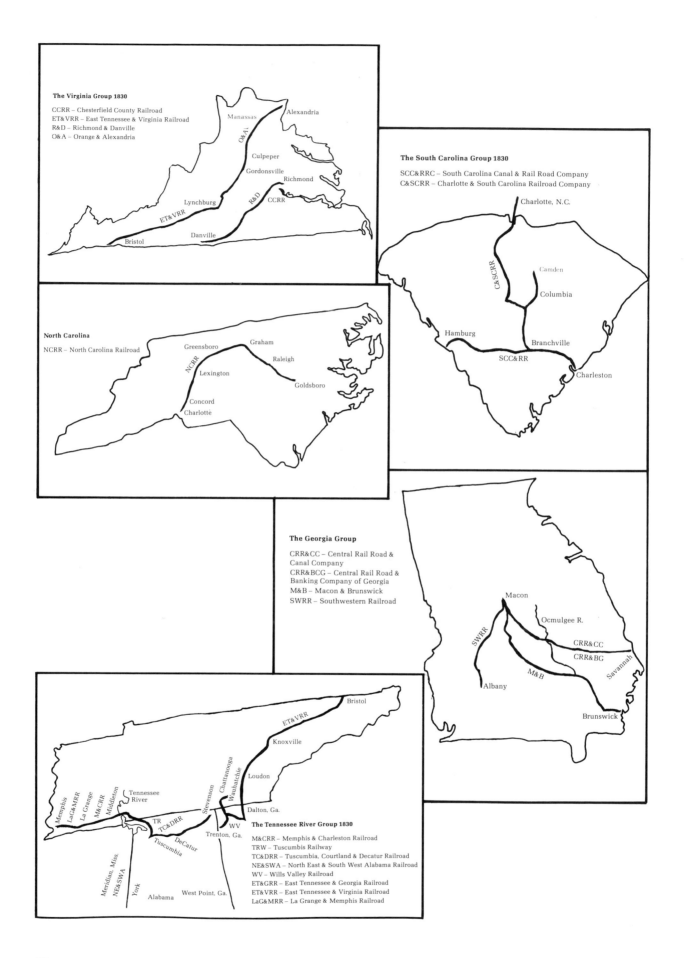

The Virginia Group 1830

CCRR – Chesterfield County Railroad
ET&VRR – East Tennessee & Virginia Railroad
R&D – Richmond & Danville
O&A – Orange & Alexandria

Alexandria
Manassas
O&A
Culpeper
Gordonsville
Richmond
Lynchburg
R&D
CCRR
ET&VRR
Danville
Bristol

The South Carolina Group 1830

SCC&RRC – South Carolina Canal & Rail Road Company
C&SCRR – Charlotte & South Carolina Railroad Company

Charlotte, N.C.
C&SCRR
Camden
Columbia
Hamburg
Branchville
SCC&RR
Charleston

North Carolina

NCRR – North Carolina Railroad

Greensboro
Graham
NCRR
Raleigh
Lexington
Goldsboro
Concord
Charlotte

The Georgia Group

CRR&CC – Central Rail Road &
Canal Company
CRR&BCG – Central Rail Road &
Banking Company of Georgia
M&B – Macon & Brunswick
SWRR – Southwestern Railroad

Macon
Ocmulgee R.
SWRR
CRR&CC
CRR&BG
M&B
Savannah
Albany
Brunswick

Bristol
ET&VRR
Knoxville
Chattanooga
Stevenson
Wauhatchie
Loudon
Dalton, Ga.
Memphis
LaG&MRR
La Grange
M&CRR
Middleton
Tennessee
River
TR
TC&DRR
WV
DeCatur
Trenton, Ga.
Tuscumbia
Meridian. Miss.
NE&SWA
York
Alabama
West Point, Ga.

The Tennessee River Group 1830

M&CRR – Memphis & Charleston Railroad
TRW – Tuscumbis Railway
TC&DRR – Tuscumbia, Courtland & Decatur Railroad
NE&SWA – North East & South West Alabama Railroad
WV – Wills Valley Railroad
ET&GRR – East Tennessee & Georgia Railroad
ET&VRR – East Tennessee & Virginia Railroad
LaG&MRR – La Grange & Memphis Railroad

A preliminary survey was commenced August 10, 1834, and in December 1835 construction was begun. The first train was operated over the entire line on October 13, 1843, and the line from Savannah to the bank of the Ocmulgee River was opened for business on November 1, 1843. Train service was operated daily thereafter, except Sundays.

Construction was begun during the administration of William Washington Gordon, its first president, but unfortunately he did not live to see the fulfillment of his vision and was succeeded by Richard R. Cuyler, who was president at the time of completion of the line to Macon.

A description of the first track construction in comparison with that of the present day will show the radical improvements which have been made.

The plan of superstructure for 100 miles from Savannah is as follows:

"Cross sleepers are first bedded in the ground rammed solid, their upper surfaces being level with the grade of the road; string pieces, six inches deep and 12 inches wide, are then trenailed flatwise on the sleepers, and the ground rammed under them, affording a continuous bearing. On the top, and in the center of these string pieces, is placed a small lath or ribbon, three by two inches of hard pine; this is surmounted by the plate or strap rail of iron, three inches wide by ¾ of an inch thick. The iron is confined by spikes seven inches long, passing through the ribbon into the string piece. Wrought iron splicing plates ¼ of an inch thick, are placed under the joinings of the bars, the spikes passing through them."

With the "Knoxville Convention" planning to build a line from Charleston to the Ohio River, the people of Georgia set about to create a rival route across Georgia and Alabama, connecting Augusta with the Mississippi River at Memphis. Moreover, the State of Georgia itself began the construction of part of this line westward from Atlanta. Meanwhile, the ambitious Louisville, Cincinnati & Charleston project failed and the people of Knoxville and East Tennessee embraced the Georgia plan by creating the Hiwassee Railroad, which was to connect Knoxville with the proposed east-west line at Dalton, Ga.

In Tennessee, a charter was granted in 1836 for the Hiwassee Railroad Company to build a connecting line with the Louisville, Cincinnati & Charleston, from Knoxville, through the Hiwassee district, to a connection with the Western & Atlantic Railroad in Georgia. (That road was part of a proposed line from Charleston to Memphis, Tenn.)

The Hiwassee failed completely and was superseded by the East Tennessee & Georgia Railroad, which actually built the line from Dalton to Loudon on the Tennessee River by August 1852, and on to Knoxville by January 1855.

While these developments were under way, another great trunk line project, this to connect the North and Southwest, was taking shape, lines being proposed from Knoxville north to Bristol and Lynchburg, Va. The East Tennessee & Georgia, with its line south from Knoxville, was in a strategic position in any development of this new north-south trunk line; hence the people of Alabama recognized the desirability of a rail connection between their own north-south Alabama & Tennessee River Railroad and the burgeoning East Tennessee & Georgia, which was figuring on "a branch line" from Cleveland, Tenn., to Chattanooga. The result was the Wills Valley Railroad, first predecessor of the Alabama Great Southern.

Although the Central Rail Road & Banking Company of Georgia was completed to the Ocmulgee River in 1843, it was not permitted to enter the City of Macon until 1851 because of opposition by the citizens. But this opposition was finally overcome and an agreement was reached by which the railroad was to pay a perpetual annuity of $5,000 to the City of Macon for the privilege of entering the city.

Upon completion of the road to Macon, it was apparent to the management that some form of transportation to the West, beyond Macon, was necessary. Accordingly, a stage line was organized to form a link in a through line from Macon to New Orleans. Arrangements were also completed to interchange traffic at Savannah with a steamer line operating between Charleston, S.C., and Savannah, thereby forming a through route from Charleston to Montgomery, Ala., and to points beyond.

Operation to Macon began in 1843, but a report by the chief engineer showed that it was not entirely finished, and while more than 114 years have elapsed, that condition still exists. (A railroad may be completed, but it is never finished while management accepts its responsibility to provide the most modern facilities developed.)

There are many interesting incidents reflected by the annual reports from the beginning of construction to the commencement of the War Between the States. In 1840, the average train speed was reduced from 22 miles per hour to 17.4 miles per hour, thereby effecting economy in maintenance due to the lower speed. In the same year, the chief engineer called attention to the greater money value of freight traffic as compared with passenger traffic, and suggested the operation of freight trains at a speed not to exceed ten miles per hour. Even in those olden days, the railroad was proud of its safety record, it being reported that for a period of seven years, subsequent to 1844, there had been no personal injury to anyone.

As far back as 1842, the officers of the railroad were statistically inclined, and it is reported that the cost of running a train per mile was 69.26 ᶜ and that fuel performance was 75.21 engine miles per cord of wood.

There was also in operation the South Carolina Canal & Rail Road Company, and the Georgia Railroad was in prospect. There was considerable competition to establish a railroad line across the State of Georgia, and lines were projected from Macon to Columbus, from Atlanta to West Point, and from a point on the Western & Atlantic Railroad to Columbus. Some of these projects materialized, and we have today the Atlanta & West Point Railroad from Atlanta to West Point, Ga., and of course other recently built railroads. But not all of these roads became a part of the Southern Railway.

When the people of East Tennessee envisioned a railroad to connect their section with eastern markets, Dr. Samuel Cunningham actively joined and eventually led the attempts to make the dream come true.

In the 1830s, when the Lynchburg and New River Railroad was chartered in Virginia, efforts were made to have it extended into Tennessee. Dr. Cunningham was on the committee that corresponded on this subject with similar groups in Tennessee and Virginia. A decade after the collapse of this early plan, the Virginia & Tennessee Railroad was successfully organized to link Lynchburg and Bristol, Va., and construction began on the East Tennessee & Georgia Railroad, running south from Knoxville. Completion of the two would leave only a 130-mile gap across upper Tennessee.

Citizens' meetings and conventions led to a charter in 1848 for the East Tennessee & Virginia Railroad, "between Knoxville and the State of Virginia, east of Bay's Mountain, between the Holston and Nolichucky Rivers." Capital was authorized in the amount of $1,500,000. Getting it was another story.

Dr. Cunningham worked tirelessly to obtain stock subscriptions for the railroad. When the charter seemed about to expire, he came forward with a plan to save it and was one of the 30 prominent East Tennessee citizens who pledged their personal fortunes to buy whatever stock was needed to save the charter, up to $500,000.

Elected first president of the East Tennessee & Virginia at the stockholders' meeting in 1849, Dr. Cunningham gave up his profitable medical practice to head the new company at a nominal salary. Against obstacles and disappointments, through financial and engineering difficulties, the sure hand of this capable surgeon led the road to completion in May 1858. A huge crowd at Keebler's field, near Midway, Tenn., cheered Dr. Cunningham as he drove the final spike. Though he gave up the presidency a year later to return to medical practice, he remained a director of the company until his death in 1867.

Meanwhile, plans for the Charlotte & South Carolina Railroad Company were begun in 1846. At the time, the South Carolina Railroad Company was operating its line from Charleston to Hamburg, with branches to Columbia and Camden, S.C., and the desire in the northern section of South Carolina for a connection with these lines which would carry the South Carolina system of railroads to Charlotte, N.C., resulted in a charter. This was granted by an act passed December 18, 1846, which provided for the organization of the Charlotte & South Carolina Railroad Company "for the purpose of establishing a communication by railroad between the States of South and North Carolina, from Charlotte in the last mentioned State, or from some point near that place to such a point on the South Carolina Railroad as may be agreed on by the stockholders."

On January 2, 1847, this was supplemented by a North Carolina franchise, but there were certain differences in the original charters in the two states, which were reconciled in a South Carolina Act passed December 19, 1848. After some hesitation in the choice of a route to a connection point with the South Carolina Railroad, between Columbia and Camden, construction was begun from Columbia in the direction of Charlotte.

From the opening of its line on October 2, 1852, the Charlotte & South Carolina Railroad was carefully and efficiently managed, and during the years before the Civil War laid a foundation of solvency which even the disaster of the Confederacy and the wrecking of the line by General Sherman could not altogether destroy. This was largely contributed to by the opening of the North Carolina Railroad to Charlotte in 1856, thus making the Charlotte & South Carolina a link in the main through line from North to South.

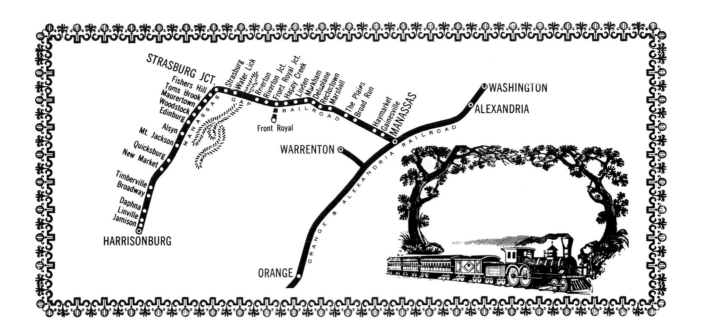

Also, in 1849, the Virginia board of public works appointed John Barbour as one of the directors of the newly organized Orange and Alexandria Railroad, in which the state had a financial interest. At this time the Orange & Alexandria, chartered in 1848 and organized early in 1849 during the upsurge of railroad interest in Virginia, had already made progress on the line from Alexandria to Gordonsville. Route surveys had been completed, 2,500 tons of 51-pound "U" rail had been bought, and the line actually opened for trains as far as Manassas.

Under Barbour's guidance, the Orange & Alexandria (O&A) grew vigorously in the decade before the Civil War. During his first year as president, the line was opened almost to Culpeper, construction began on the Warrenton branch and the company received a contract to carry the United States Mail. Already Barbour was looking ahead to an extension of the O&A line, to a connection with the Virginia & Tennessee line at Lynchburg, and by the middle of 1853 had surveys under way to locate a route.

To the building of the North Carolina Railroad in the early 1850s, John Motley Morehead brought a limitless personal enthusiasm and the public confidence and respect needed to unite the state. Morehead was a commanding figure in North Carolina public life of the period. He had combined a successful career as an attorney with the able leadership of several business enterprises. At different times, he had represented two counties in the state legislature and had won the first popular election for governor.

Divided opinion in the state on the need for the proposed railroad put such enthusiasm and leadership at a premium. In the new western counties, railroad fever ran high and had for a decade or more. But the older, more settled tidewater regions of North Carolina had reasonably good transportation for the time (including two north-south railroads) and felt little inclination to spend large sums for the project.

What gave the North Carolina railroad idea a chance in the 1848-49 session of the state legislature was the growing concern that the developing Virginia railroads might soon extend to drain away the trade and commerce of western North Carolina. Even so, the bill to charter the North Carolina Railroad Company ran into difficulties in the state senate. Final voting on the charter bill on January 28, 1849, ended in a tie of 22 for and 22 against. Calvin Graves, temporary speaker, had to cast the deciding vote. He was a Democrat from Caswell County. Both his party and his constituents opposed the railroad. Though his political future hung in the balance, he didn't hesitate — "The chair decides in the affirmative."

But the North Carolina Railroad Company thus existed only on paper. Its authorization to build a line from Goldsboro, through Raleigh and Salisbury, to Charlotte meant little without financial backing and able leadership. The charter set capital stock at $3 million, of which the state was to take $2 million as soon as the other million had been subscribed by private capital and one-half the amount actually paid. John M. Morehead, of Greensboro, led the effort to close the million-dollar gap between a paper charter and a railroad.

One of 15 commissioners named to put the railroad act into effect, Morehead was also placed in charge of the Greensboro subcommittee, to open books there for stock subscriptions in the new road. But more than that, he became the railroad's eloquent advocate throughout the state, lending to the project his own considerable reputation. In April 1849, he addressed a railroad meeting at Raleigh, and another in May near what is now High Point. He was elected to preside at the state-wide railroad convention at Salisbury in June, at which time the subscription books for stock were opened.

At the second state-wide railroad convention at Greensboro, less than $200,000 had been subscribed, and that almost entirely in the western counties. To obtain the remaining $800,000, there was a proposal to persuade 100 men or corporations to subscribe the balance. John Morehead came forward to head a list of 51 men who agreed to take such "shares." Now the railroad needed 49 more like them.

For the meeting in Goldsboro, which he was unable to attend, the railroad's enthusiast penned a moving appeal: "It is truly the great redeeming improvement that is to make us one people, one state, one great community . . . The Road Must Be Built . . ."

When the third railroad convention met at Hillsboro in February 1850, the full 100 shares were pledged. But it was discovered that in the process the original stock subscriptions had shrunk to little more than $100,000. Refusing to be discouraged, Morehead offered to head another list of ten men to take $10,000 worth of stock each to make up the difference. With the full million pledged, stockholders met at Salisbury on July 11, 1850, to organize the company. They elected directors, who promptly named John M. Morehead the company's first president and engaged Walter Gwynn as chief engineer.

Engineering surveys, reported to the stockholders at their second annual meeting in May 1851, indicated that a route through or near the towns of Hillsboro, Graham, Greensboro, Lexington and Concord would be practical. (Many of the stock subscriptions depended on such a route.) The chief engineer estimated the cost at close to $3.5 million, including equipment and shops.

Ground was first broken for the new line at Greensboro on July 11, 1851. Appropriately, President Morehead introduced Calvin Graves to turn the first spadeful of earth. Grading contracts for the whole distance had been let, principally to stockholders, with the work to begin the next January (1852). Contractors were to be paid half in cash and half in stock. Actually, they received nothing at all the first year. President Morehead called it "an anomaly in railroad building — do the work first and receive the means to do it afterwards."

With their own resources, the contractors finished a half-million dollars' worth of grading in 1852. Applied to stock credits, this sum was enough to authorize the state to take $2 million worth of stock.

The company let a private contract for construction of the Goldsboro-Raleigh portion of the line, but undertook with its own forces to lay track between Raleigh and Charlotte. Starts were made from each end, but the work went slowly. By July 1854, the work under private contract was complete, but only a few miles of track extended from Charlotte and from Raleigh. Increasing prices of material pushed up the cost estimate, and President Morehead had to go to the legislature for another million-dollar stock subscription.

By the time Morehead turned in his resignation in July 1855, the road was nearing completion. The first through trains ran on January 30, 1856.

While the grading work was being done on the North Carolina Railroad, the Wills Valley was being chartered (February 3, 1852) to build a line from the farm of James Hamton (on the Alabama & Tennessee River Railroad), through DeKalb County, to an intersection with the East Tennessee & Georgia Railroad "at some convenient point in Lookout Valley." It was later found that the existing line of the Nashville & Chattanooga Railroad (now part of the CSX Corp.) proved an entrance into Chattanooga, and the Wills Valley therefore began construction of its line from Wauhatchie, Tenn. (on the Memphis & Charleston), south to Trenton, Ga., in 1860. This 12-mile line was operated throughout the war.

A year after the Wills Valley was chartered, it was decided to extend its lines southwesterly to a connection with the proposed trunk line to run from West Point, Ga., across Alabama and Mississippi, to the Mississippi River. The result was the chartering on December 12, 1853, of the North East & South West Alabama Railroad, the second of the predecessor lines of the Alabama Great Southern.

The North East & South West Alabama began building its line northeastward from Meridian to York, Ala., a distance of 27 miles being completed when the war broke out.

By 1854, the Orange & Alexandria reached Gordonsville. The Lynchburg extension was well under way in 1855 and was averaging more than $20,000 a month. In connection with the Virginia Central, the company made a successful bid for the profitable mail route between Washington and Richmond.

The expenses of the Lynchburg extension began to put a serious strain on the company's resources in 1857. The work stopped briefly at the end of that year, but was resumed a few months later at the prospect of a loan from the state. As fast as the company's means permitted, it was pushed toward the Virginia & Tennessee connection to give Virginia a rail connection with the Mobile and Orleans.

Completion of the last section of the James River Bridge opened the Orange & Alexandria's route to Lynchburg later in 1860. That year it seemed that John Barbour headed a company with fine prospects.

The opening of the North Carolina Railroad from Raleigh to Goldsboro, N.C., in 1856 effected a connection between the South Carolina and Virginia railroads through the Charlotte & South Carolina Railroad, which in 1852 had extended the South Carolina system north from Columbia to Charlotte.

In the mid-1850s, more than a quarter of the state of Georgia had only rivers and poor roads for transport. So, while riding the rutted roads of the Brunswick judicial circuit, Judge Arthur E. Cochran had more than enough opportunity to feel the need for better transportation in a wide area of South Georgia.

To the north of his circuit ran the well-established Central of Georgia Railroad, from Macon to Savannah. To the west lay the Southwestern Railroad, from Macon to Albany. The Savannah, Albany & Gulf Railroad semicircled it on the southeast. The Central of Georgia Railroad channeled most of the traffic from the interior to the coast at Savannah. People in the port of Brunswick were eager for their own rail connection with Central Georgia and the territory beyond.

To realize his railroad plan, Judge Cochran resigned from the bench and successfully sought election to the state senate. He is believed to have drafted the bill that gave the Macon & Brunswick its original charter in March 1856. Cochran's name was not among those listed in the charter as incorporators. Yet, when the group met in June 1857 to form a temporary organization of the company, he was unanimously elected its first president.

The state charter was accepted and the company's capital stock was set at $400,000. Records of the meeting also indicate that at least a preliminary survey of the route had already been made.

On December 17, 1857, the state legislature amended the company's charter to increase and define more clearly its powers and privileges. An increase in capital stock to $2 million was authorized. One day later, the road's board of directors met to plan ways to raise the $200,000 in stock subscriptions required before the company could be formally organized.

Cochran was appointed agent to secure subscriptions in the counties near Brunswick. His fellow directors of the Brunswick & Florida Railroad agreed for use of that company's track into Brunswick.

Raising money for the road apparently occupied most of the director's energies in 1858. By early 1859, more than a half-million dollars in stock had been pledged, more than enough to allow formal organization under the charter. The directors again named Cochran as president; they would do so every year until his death in 1865.

Cochran's report on the road's first year of growth, sent to stockholders in February 1860, breathed a heady optimism. A chief engineer had been selected. He was Major E. McNeill, who made the original route survey of the entire line, which had been tentatively located by the end of June.

"Pay as you go" was to be the rule on the Macon & Brunswick, Cochran assured the stockholders. The directors had let contracts for grading of no more road than they believed could be built and paid for with the subscriptions in hand.

Since most of the stock pledges, some due in 1860 and some in 1861, came from individuals and cities at the two ends of the proposed route, the railroad would be built from the ends toward the middle. By October 1859, contracts had been let for grading 66½ miles out of Macon along the east side of the Ocmulgee River and 29 miles from a point on the Brunswick & Florida Railroad 11 miles from Brunswick.

Cochran believed that if these two sections alone could be completed, they would pay for themselves. But he also believed and told the stockholders that the completion of the entire line (estimated cost of $2 million) must come, and that such a line would channel valuable trade from the mid-South to Macon, Brunswick and the whole South Georgia area.

"For this line must and will be established if the Union stands, and if it is dissolved, it will become an absolute necessity for the South."

Events in 1860 seemed to justify his optimism. By the time of the second annual report, in February 1861, grading extended for 35 miles out of Macon, with track laid on 20 miles of it and a train running. This was a construction train, powered by the line's only locomotive, but it carried an accommodation car for passengers.

Iron for the rest of the northern division awaited delivery upriver from the port, and the line was expected to be graded and ready to receive it by mid-summer. Grading on the southern division outside of Brunswick lacked only two miles to completion.

The company had accepted an offer of $121,000 in stock pledges from the citizens of Hawkinsville, Ga., in return for the promise of a ten-mile branch from the main line to that point. Route surveys had already started.

In the separation of the Union into two parts, the Macon & Brunswick's president foresaw a new and vital need for the railroad they were building: ". . . A new government is soon to be formed by a Union of the Southern Slaveholding states. Georgia is the commercial, as well as the geographical centre of the Confederation, and Macon is the centre of Georgia. Brunswick is the best, and only suitable port for the establishment of a Navy Yard and Ship-Building combined . . ."

Meanwhile, the Memphis & Charleston Railroad Company (now Southern's Memphis division) had been chartered and had absorbed the old La Grange & Memphis and the Tuscumbia, Courtland & Decatur railroads. Its purpose was to complete a line from Memphis to a connection with the Nashville & Chattanooga Railroad at Stevenson, Ala., and thus perfect the final link in a through system of railroads from the Atlantic Ocean to the Mississippi. When the Memphis & Charleston laid the last rail to complete the road in 1857, a South-wide celebration at Memphis hailed the opening of the 759-mile line, the longest connected system of railroads then in existence.

Railroad spirit continued strong in Knoxville. The East Tennessee & Virginia Railroad was organized to build a line north and east toward Virginia. After some difficulties, a line was opened from Knoxville to Bristol in October 1858. Until the outbreak of the Civil War, this was operated as a through line with the East Tennessee & Georgia (Dalton to Knoxville) and the Virginia & Tennessee (Bristol to Lynchburg — it did not become part of the Southern).

The busy river port and cotton planters' capital of Memphis, Tenn., in 1857 was literally "bustin' at the seams" with the pioneer vigor that sent thousands of Americans westward across the old boundaries into the great frontier. Foundations for new buildings were being laid at night by gaslight, so pressing was the demand for new stores, offices and homes. But when a new railroad pushed through to link the Mississippi River with the Atlantic port of Charleston, even busy Memphis had to take time out to celebrate. Highlight of the two-day railroad jubilee was an unusual but enduring wedding ceremony — "The Marriage of the Waters." Water brought from the Atlantic, off Charleston, S.C., was sprayed into the Mississippi in token of the completion of the Memphis & Charleston Railroad, the final link in a through rail route between the Atlantic Ocean and the Mississippi River, steamboat highway of the continent.

The matchmakers, so to speak, were five railroads: the Memphis & Charleston, which operated from Memphis to Stevenson, Ala.; the Nashville & Chattanooga Railroad, from Stevenson to Chattanooga, Tenn.; the Western & Atlantic, from there to Atlanta; the Georgia Railroad, from Atlanta to Augusta; and the South Carolina Railroad, from there to Charleston.

Connecting the Atlantic port of Charleston with the Mississippi River meant the realization of a 20-year dream of the pioneer railroaders of the South, a link between the Atlantic Seaboard and the fast-developing mid-South and Southwest.

Memphis had completely succumbed to the prevailing railroad fever more than a decade earlier, when a great commercial convention in that city in 1854 cheered the idea of railroads extending from the Bluff City to both oceans.

Public enthusiasm for the railroads undoubtedly helped Colonel Samuel Tate, destined to become president of the road, push through the construction of the Memphis & Charleston (M&C) where similar enterprises (namely the La Grange & Memphis and the Tuscumbia, Courtland & Decatur) had been unable to complete the entire route. Chartered in 1846, the M&C really got under way two years later when it was further authorized to acquire the chartered route surveyed by the Memphis & La Grange Railroad and the already constructed line of the Tuscumbia, Courtland & Decatur (by that time it had been reorganized as the Tennessee Valley Railroad Company.)

By 1852, the road was graded as far as La Grange, Tenn., trains were running to Collierville and the right-of-way for the Memphis & Charleston through Mississippi and Alabama had been obtained. By 1855, the railroad was in operation for 70 miles, from Memphis to Middleton, Tenn., and Colonel Tate had announced the purchase of enough iron (7,500 tons) to complete the entire line.

Even in its partially completed stage, the new railroad gave proof of its future worth as a commercial artery for the city. For example, the amount of cotton carried by the M&C increased from 56,875 bales in 1854 to 98,908 bales in 1856.

Excitement mounted through the early months of 1857 as the road neared completion. Through tickets were being sold to Augusta and Charleston (passengers bridged the narrowing gap in the track by means of fast stagecoaches). As the workmen put in the last miles of track, front-page advertisements in the Memphis *Daily Appeal* kept pace with ringing sledges. "Open to Corinth, staging reduced to 40 miles." "Open to Burns, staging reduced to 12 miles." And finally on April 1 the boldface letters "Completed."

President Samuel Tate had pledged to the stockholders that the road would be open by April 1. Actually, the deadline was met with several days to spare. On March 28, Senator James C. Jones, ex-governor of Tennessee and an ardent railroad enthusiast, drove the last spike to complete the railroad. The mayor and aldermen of Memphis resolved on a public celebration of the event, to take place on May 1. As it turned out, one day wasn't nearly enough. The "Great Railroad Jubilee" lasted two days in Memphis alone and was marked by later celebrations in Atlanta, Macon, Charleston and Savannah. The road to the West lay open!

Memphis went all out to celebrate the new railroad era. In the early dawn of May 1, an artillery battery on the bluff near Memphis sent echoes rolling down the muddy shores of the Mississippi. Later in the morning, a mile-long procession began to form on upper Main Street. Visitors from every state in the South helped to swell to 30,000 the crowd that jammed the streets, packed the balconies and wooden awnings, or vied for places at the shop windows of Memphis.

Headed by military companies, bands and fire companies — among them Charleston's Phoenix Fire Company, with their engine and two hogsheads of Atlantic Ocean brine brought from Charleston for the celebration — the procession made its way through flag-decked streets to Court Square. In the parade were schoolchildren in May Day costumes and carriages bearing visiting mayors, aldermen, city officials of Memphis and other distinguished guests.

A crowd in high good humor applauded speeches by President Samuel Tate of the Memphis & Charleston, Mayor A.H. Douglas of Memphis and Mayor William P. Miles of Charleston. (As a bachelor, Mayor Miles took a full measure of good-natured ribbing about the "marriage of the waters" during the celebration.)

The 10,000 guests made their way to the quarter-mile-long tables that had been set up at the Navy Yard for a picnic-style dinner. There was dancing that night at the Navy yard and fireworks burst and glared on the bluff opposite Madison Street.

With the ball at the Exchanges Building, the visitors thronged in the street till dawn and the triumphal arch at Main and Madison streets was aglow with flickering gaslight. Night became a colorful prelude to the ceremony to be held the next day at the river.

Long before the appointed hour on May 2, people swarmed over the bluff, the wharf and the decks of river steamers, growing more and more restless as the parade from Court Square failed to arrive. Finally, the marchers appeared, with the Phoenix Fire Company and their engine in the lead. When the orators were finished, the fire engine went into action. With firemen manning the engine and a dignitary holding the nozzle, the muddy Father of Waters and the Atlantic Ocean were officially united by a spray of salt water that glittered like a shower of diamonds as it burst from the nozzle and arched into the Mississippi River.

Following the ceremony, there was an excursion up the river in five palatial steamboats, a fitting close to an eventful day. Later that evening, there was a banquet where local newspapermen gathered with visiting press representatives and other guests to toast the various states represented and the new railroad era that was beginning.

The celebrations would soon come to an end, because there was growing unrest in the South. These new railroads would soon be put to the supreme test, as the hour was late and the clouds of war were gathering on the horizon . . . .

Drawing of a Manassas Gap train carrying troops to Manassas Junction to aid in the Battle of First Manassas.

- Norfolk Southern Corp.

Chapter II

The War Years
1860 – 1865

Railroads that were later to become part of the Southern System were spreading throughout the South as the nineteenth century reached and passed its midpoint. In Alabama, Georgia, Tennessee, the Carolinas and Virginia, iron rails were reaching out to open new territory to commerce and industry.

In the struggle that bitterly divided the American nation, much of the South became a battlefield. And the South's railroads were in the thick of the fighting.

Leaders on both sides soon recognized the vital military importance of railroads. Some of the first military action was directed against this highly useful form of transportation.

Shells from the Charleston water batteries arched into Fort Sumter in the spring of 1861, and the railroads of the South went to war on April 18, 1861. They would remain in the struggle until the end.

On April 17, 1861, the State of Virginia seceded from the Union, thus casting its lot with the Confederacy. No one knew on the morning of April 18, 1861, when three trains clattered into the village from the South, that soon their village would be caught up in heavy fighting in the Battle of First Manassas.

If here and there throughout Manassas Junction a man could be heard to disclaim the morning's events as general madness, pure and simple, he could hardly be blamed, because what the villagers of Manassas Junction saw that April morning had never before been seen. That morning, the Orange & Alexandria and the Manassas Gap railroads were handmaidens to history. For the first time anywhere, railroads were being employed tactically to move troops and artillery in a direct assault maneuver against an enemy-held strong point.

The men aboard the trains knew they were on their way to battle. They were on their way to attack and expected to capture the Federal arsenal at Harper's Ferry, important not only as a prize source of badly needed arms and ammunition but also as the gateway to the Shenandoah Valley, a natural north-south route running between the Blue Ridge and the Allegheny foothills into the heartland of the proud new Confederacy of Southern States.

About midnight, the infantry units, and the Fauquier and Clarke County cavalry groups which had then joined them, began an cautious advance on the arsenal. They advanced toward disappointment. The arsenal at Harper's Ferry was already in flames and had been since nine that evening. But the expedition could not be termed unsuccessful, even though dawn on the 19th revealed the very discouraging sight of 20,000 fire-destroyed weapons, which the raiders had hoped to place in the hands of the growing Confederate forces. An important Federal point had been taken, thereby providing a marshalling place for the 1,300 Virginia volunteers who would gather there within a week, and some machinery of value was salvaged from the ruins.

Later, Confederate troops operating out of Harper's Ferry were to seize and ship to the South numbers of railroad locomotives and cars which were to help immeasurably in sustaining their cause. This equipment would find its way south over the same railroads that the original Harper's Ferry raiders had used, the Manassas Gap and the Orange & Alexandria.

War turned the peaceful territory served by the Orange & Alexandria into a flaming battleground. Five years of it strained the Orange & Alexandria almost to the breaking point. Laden with the military traffic of both armies, dismembered and divided between the Confederacy and the Union, fought over, wrecked and ravaged, the O&A continued to operate with increasing difficulty throughout the war years.

John S. Barbour seldom knew with any certainty from one month to the next just how much railroad he would be president of at any given time. His own reports to the stockholders during that period gave a graphic picture of "Rails Across A Battleground":

1861 — "The invasion of the territory of the State and occupation of the City of Alexandria by the Federal troops on the 24th of May last deprived the company of its established general offices, disturbed its regular system of auditing accounts, and necessarily produced much confusion in the management of its business.

"Transportation of troops and military stores since the act of secession had afforded a very large business, and taxed to its utmost capacity the somewhat limited equipment of the road.

"Since the 24th of May last, the road has not been operated by the regular passenger trains, beyond Manassas station.

"Sections of the track were destroyed and the bridges burned from Cameron to Bull Run, and 22 miles of the railroad, in the direction nearest to Alexandria, surrendered to the control of the enemy or rendered useless to the company."

On July 21, 1861, just three months after the raid on Harper's Ferry, the Manassas Gap and the Orange & Alexandria transported Confederate soldiers to the Southern victory that would be known as the Battle of First Manassas.

Troop movement by rail to this battlefield made even more evident rail's military advantages — first indicated by the use Captain Imboden's raiders had made of the Virginia Central, Orange & Alexandria, Manassas Gap, and the Winchester & Potomac. The impartial railroad locomotive would respond to the touch of whatever hand should stroke it.

Most of the battles of the Civil War involved struggles for the control of railroad lines. The collapse of the Confederacy was hastened as it lost control of more and more rail mileage, and as the lines it continued to control deteriorated under wartime shortages of material and the inability to replace locomotives and cars.

The first major clash between Union and Confederate armies erupted on the rolling plains of Manassas, some 26 miles from Washington, on July 21, 1861. It ended with the North in a headlong retreat over roads already clogged with fleeing civilian sightseers who had come out earlier in carriages, some with picnic lunches, "to watch the show."

The turning point in the all-day battle came with the arrival over the Manassas Gap Railroad of Confederate reinforcements from Piedmont, a station on the railroad just east of the Blue Ridge. Undaunted by the hazards of the three-hour-long, pell-mell ride eastward through the Bull Run Mountains, while crowded into and on top of railroad boxcars, the fresh Confederate troops came up to shatter the strong Union right. With its collapse, the rest of the Union line was shortly thrown into panic-stricken flight.

The moment of victory came suddenly.

Union forces rode a favoring tide in the battle at three o'clock in the afternoon. After hours of seesaw fighting, during which first one side then the other came within a hair of victory, it seemed at last that Union General Irvin McDowell's men would claim the day. But before another hour had passed, the Union army was fleeing the field ahead of Southern bayonets.

Throughout the entire battle, there was no more timely arrival on the field than that of the 6th North Carolina. Marching straight from their boxcars into the Union right, the men of the 6th topped an obscuring rise to find themselves facing the strongest point in the Union line — two batteries of cannons which throughout the afternoon had anchored McDowell's right securely to the field.

Commanded by Captains Charles Griffin and James B. Ricketts, the batteries' deadly fire had cut down one Confederate advance after another. It was around these two batteries that the seesaw battle mainly swirled — they reportedly changed hands three times during the day — and it was charging them behind fixed bayonets and clearing them of their Union defenders by the men of the 6th North Carolina that decided the day.

Colonel Charles Frederick Fisher, commander of the 6th, was so anxious to have a hand in the battle that he fell dead in the fierce contest for the cannons.

Shortly afterwards, Kirby Smith's Confederate forces arrived from Piedmont over the Manassas Gap and consolidated the Confederate positions on the Union right.

Then, gradually, the Union began to give way all down the line. Each inch of ground reluctantly surrendered was doggedly occupied by the Confederates. Soon the ground was given in feet. Then in yards. So the retreat went — as far as Bull Run.

As retreat carried them across that muddy stream, panic struck the Union army. Weapons were abandoned. Horses were cut from their traces and ridden wildly off. Sightseers were thrown from their carriages by frantic Union soldiers. To pause but briefly meant being trampled underfoot.

The Memphis and Charleston Ry. station at Corinth, Miss. — *Norfolk Southern Corp.*

View of roundhouse, Alexandria, Va., Orange & Alexandria Railroad during the War Between the States. — *Norfolk Southern Corp.*

Wrecks were a frequent occurrence on the O&A during the war years. Part of it was operated by Federal forces as the U.S. Military RR., part operated for the Confederacy. It was a railroad divided.
– *Norfolk Southern Corp.*

The 13-inch mortar shown was named "The Dictator." It was used by the Federal artillery around Petersburg during the closing months of the war.
– *Norfolk Southern Corp.*

Another Civil War first was the development of rail-carried mortars like this one used in the Virginia campaigns.
– *Norfolk Southern Corp.*

Atlanta was a Confederate rail center. It was served by three of the five through rail routes of the South in 1860.
– *Norfolk Southern Corp.*

Railroad depot at Chattanooga, Tenn., taken during the War. A Southern rail center, Chattanooga was located on two of the five through rail routes in the South in 1860.

- Norfolk Southern Corp.

Nor did the Union hold Centreville, nor stop in Alexandria. On into Washington, across the Long Bridge, went the same men who had set out from that same place a few weeks earlier in confident expectation that Richmond would soon be their prize.

The Southern forces that were involved in the Battle of First Manassas were: the 33rd and 17th Virginia, 5th and 6th North Carolina, 7th and 8th Georgia Regiments, 2nd and 4th Alabama, and the 11th Mississippi.

After the battle of July 21, President Barbour of the Orange & Alexandria told the stockholders: "The streams between Manassas and Fairfax Station were temporarily bridged again by order of our military authorities, for use of the army only, but recently this part of the line has again been abandoned . . .

"Notwithstanding all the damage incurred, it is some satisfaction to the stockholders of the company to know that, but for the construction and existence of this railroad, the state could not have been defended as it has been . . .

"The annals of railroad operations do not anywhere exhibit examples of such continuous laborious service as have been performed for months together by the men who have run the trains to and from Manassas Station, and transacted the business of the road at that place. Without a house to shelter them from the weather, poorly supplied with necessary food, and the impossibility of obtaining assistance for their relief, by day and by night they have stood to their posts without complaint and performed an amount of work scarcely to be conceived as within the compass of human efforts."

On the Orange & Alexandria, Barbour told the stockholders in 1863 that "several of the principal bridges of the company across the Rappahannock and Rapidan, and minor streams, have been destroyed during the year, either by our own military authorities or those of the enemy. Most of these, however, have been renewed by temporary structures so as to admit the crossing of trains. The enemy has also relaid a considerable portion of the track in Prince William and Fauquier counties, destroyed by order of General Johnson upon the retreat of his forces from Manassas last Spring, and has also put down extensive sidings at several points. With the exception of the break, for want of a bridge at Broad Run, nearly the whole line of railroad from Gordonsville to Alexandria is now run by one side or the other. The regular passenger trains do not now pass beyond Culpeper Courthouse."

In 1864, due to "the advancing and receding waves of military operations, much of the bridging and line of railroad east of the Rappahannock River have been destroyed. The damage however has been generally repaired by the enemy . . .

"The Confederate States has ceased to pay its transportation in bonds for some months past, and now pays in Treasury notes . . . the company will have on hand to dispose of, since the payment of the debt to the Richmond, Fredericksburg and Potomac Company, about $100,000 in Confederate bonds and $200,000 in money, without anticipating further receipts."

When artillery first took to the rails, it was on the tracks of the Richmond & York River Railroad. The Richmond & York River Railroad was too young to go to war.

The 39-mile-long line of road from Richmond east to West Point on the York River had been open less than a month when Virginia's secession from the Union in April 1861 made it fair game for ravaging. When the tide of the Civil War finally flooded down upon it, what one side did not destroy the other did. The hapless little railroad was literally wiped from the face of the earth, as along its right-of-way (now part of the Southern Railway's Richmond division) occurred some of the most decisive, bloodiest fighting in the war.

But in the process, the railroad made history. It was upon the tracks of this Southern predecessor that the world first saw the use of mobile artillery mounted on railroad trucks.

Throughout the first year of the war, as was noted in the annual report for the fiscal year ending September 30, 1861, the Richmond & York River was "chiefly employed in the aid of the war of independence which the South was waging, by the transportation of troops and the various things necessary to equip and support them."

But abruptly, in the spring of 1862, Union General George B. McClellan came with 90,000 men to sit astraddle the railroad and put Richmond under siege.

The man in command of the Confederate forces facing McClellan was General Robert E. Lee, and his position was not to be envied.

Threatened by Union invasion in eastern North Carolina, faced with the reality of Union penetration in Alabama, stymied on the Mississippi River by Union gunboats, the Confederacy seemed tottering. New Orleans had fallen, and now Richmond itself — the very keystone of the Confederacy's tenacious perseverance — was a besieged capital.

In the Richmond yards of the Richmond & Danville Railroad (another Southern predecessor), an engine stood constantly under a full head of steam, able to move immediately to carry out its assigned mission of hauling the Confederate treasury to a safe place if Union troops finally entered the city.

Throughout April and May, the R&D had been dismantling its Richmond shops and shipping the vital machinery to safety at Danville.

The situation demanded extraordinary talents, exactly the sort which General Robert E. Lee possessed. He knew the tools of war and how best to apply them. And high on the list of those tools which he considered well-fitted to war were the railroads. He had watched with interest the evacuation of the wounded from the Battle of Fair Oaks over the tracks of the Richmond & York River on May 31. He knew from the lesson of First Manassas that such an operation would test a railroad's capabilities severely.

The railroad in that case had been the Orange & Alexandria. It had been the first railroad in history to remove wounded men from a battlefield.

Four days after assuming command of the Confederate forces at Richmond, Lee wrote to Colonel Josiah Gorgas, chief of Confederate ordnance, with a novel proposal. "Is there a possibility," he asked in his letter of June 5, 1862, "of constructing an iron-plated battery, mounting a heavy gun on a truck, the whole covered with iron, to move along the York River railroad? Please see what can be done. If a proper one can be got up at once, it will be of immense advantage to us . . . ."

The Union lines formed up before Richmond, along both sides of the Richmond & York River. A large cannon placed on the road's tracks could thus be run right down the Yankees' throats as the wedge for a Confederate assault, Lee thought.

In a letter dated June 24, 1862, one day before the start of what was to be known as the Seven Days' Battles, Lee was advised by Captain George Minor of Confederate ordnance: "The railroad iron-plated battery designed by Lt. John M. Brooke, C.S. Navy, has been completed. The gun, a rifled and banded 32 pounder of 57 cwt (6,384 pounds), has been mounted and equipped by Lt. R.D. Minor, C.S. Navy, and with 200 rounds of ammunition, including a 15 inch solid bolt shot, is now ready to be transferred to the army."

What Historian Louis Manarin calls "the earliest railroad artillery of record" was ready to go, and five days later, June 29, it was in action on the Richmond & York River tracks at Savage's Station, about 10 miles from Richmond. Those five days had seen the Union siege broken in a series of bloody battles that had sent the Federals reeling southward toward the James under the repeated blows of Lee's iron-plated railroad battery and his Confederate troops.

When the Seven Days' Battles ended, the siege of Richmond had been lifted. Lee was able to regroup his Army of Northern Virginia and turn north in a series of offensives that ended on a Pennsylvania field at Gettysburg in July 1863.

The Memphis & Charleston Railroad (now Southern's Memphis division) had been in full operation for only four years, a four-year ordeal by fire.

This story of a Southern predecessor line's war years — its "portrait in powder smoke" — was made possible because Sam Tate, builder and wartime president of the M&C, told it in his careful accounting to the stockholders at the war's end. It was their first meeting in five years and President Tate felt that the owners of the property ought to know just what had happened in the meantime.

"Vital east-west artery of the Confederacy, the Memphis & Charleston received the personal attention of Yank and Johnny Reb alike . . . It was, Tate reported with some bitterness, "practically the picket line of both armies, and each seeming to vie with each other to see which one could produce the greatest amount of destruction to your property."

Though the Memphis & Charleston began to feel the press of war as early as 1861, and military officers frequently took control of trains, the real ordeal of the road began in April 1862.

In a thrust aimed at cutting the Memphis & Charleston near Corinth, Miss., the new Federal general, U.S. Grant, was trapped, with most of his Army of the Tennessee, at Pittsburg Landing, Tenn. In a two-day battle centering around Shiloh Church, the Union forces smashed their way out of the trap and drove the Confederates back to entrenchments around Corinth. Five days later, on April 11, a large Federal army took Huntsville, Ala.

President Tate told the stockholders in the spring of 1862 "that the Federal Army descended on Huntsville, Ala., and captured the railroad at that point. With all its shops, rolling stock, offices, books, material and valuable property, including 18 locomotives, 100 freight cars, six passenger cars, two baggage and a large number of road and hand cars, all your shop tools and material at Huntsville, and a large amount of wood."

War torn Atlanta, Ga., during the War Between the States.

- Norfolk Southern Corp.

United States military railroad yards at Alexandria, Va., in 1863. Note the various types of cars and locomotives and the hospital car.

- Norfolk Southern Corp.

Immediately, the Confederate commander ordered all available rolling stock and equipment moved west of Corinth. With equal speed the Federal forces maneuvered to cut off this movement. Corinth remained under siege for a month and a half. The road, its rolling stock and its men were strained to the limit. A decisive battle was expected, but none came. Instead, on May 29, a sudden order came to evacuate Corinth and the railroad.

President Tate said, "The order was to remove everything by 12 o'clock that night, that the troops would leave the entrenchments at that hour. The large amount of property to remove, the short time allowed for its removal, rendered it impossible to execute the order without great confusion and serious loss.

"The commanding General of the Confederate forces ordered all your rolling stock and other valuable property to be removed from the line of your road, down the Mobile & Ohio and Mississippi Central Roads. It was done in obedience to that order, the last seven trains leaving Corinth at 4 o'clock on the morning of May 30, 1862, where they were detained by the military authorities."

That delay proved fatal. Chugging west 13 miles to Cypress Creek, trainmen on the last few trains discovered the bridge aflame and impassable, their escape route cut off. After ordering the bridge burned, the Confederate commander had not warned the railway officers. Rather than let the equipment fall into enemy hands, the military ordered it destroyed.

"By this misfortune you lost four of your best engines and over 30 cars. This, together with your losses at Huntsville and a large number of cars smashed up and lost in so heavy an accumulation of stock at Corinth, reduced your rolling stock very materially.

"After moving everything that I could get away under the orders I had received," Tate reported, "and arranging the business of the company as best I could . . . I proceeded south with this stock and all the assets of this company that I could get together.

"We located at Marion, Miss., where we erected temporary shops, and began putting the machinery in order; but finding as fast as we could put an engine or car in order it was ordered away by the military, I finally abandoned the project and procured authority from the military to make contracts for, and receive hire from, the various Roads on which your machinery had been ordered.

"In the fall of 1862, after the evacuation of your Road by the Federal army, from Decatur to Stevenson, by order of General Bragg the Board again resumed its possession, rebuilt the Road between those points, and a portion of the shop machinery, all of which had been destroyed or badly damaged.

"As soon as rebuilt, they operated this portion of the Road until July 1, 1863, when they were again forced to evacuate by order of General Bragg, taking south what little machinery they had left.

"From this time until the close of the war, your property, or most of it, remained in the hands of the Federal army, being constantly raided upon by the Confederates."

After repairing what machinery was left, the shop at Marion, Miss., was abandoned and headquarters of the railway was moved to Demoplis, Ala. There the president, general superintendent and treasurer tried to hold the shell of the railway together. They prepared monthly accounts, tried to collect what was owed the railway and invest the funds as best they could.

As the conflict wore on into 1864 and 1865, collections became difficult, then impossible. The hard-pressed Confederate government could not pay the other roads promptly for transportation service. They, in turn, could not pay the M&C for equipment rentals.

In the final collapse of the Confederacy, the demoralized condition of the country and the numerous Federal raids made life and the safety of property a hazardous matter.

"It was hard to tell what was best to do, or where to go for safety," Tate recalled. "Your books and valuable assets were kept in [the] charge of Mr. Robertson, your Treasurer, who acted under my immediate direction, and moved from place to place as circumstances seemed to justify for safety.

"I made numerous efforts to get your more valuable assets to Canada or Europe, and succeeded in sending to Liverpool over $300,000 of Tennessee bonds. The remainder of the assets were kept South until after General Lee and Johnston's surrender. A few days before General Taylor's surrender, I succeeded in getting them to a steamer on the Yazoo River, and sent them to St. Louis, where I afterward took possession of them.

"Immediately after General Taylor's surrender, I passed into the Federal lines and proceeded to Washington, and procured a special amnesty and pardon from the President restoring me to my rights of citizenship."

President Sam Tate was thus in a position to ask for the return of the property to its prewar owners and to reorganize the company with a board of directors acceptable to the Federal government. This he did at a special meeting of stockholders in July 1865.

The needs of the war in 1862 dictated the building of a railroad that commercial rivalries between the states of Virginia and North Carolina had prevented for years. The Piedmont Railroad bridged the 52 miles between Danville, Va., and Greensboro, N.C., to give the Confederacy a through line of interior railroad communications. Built by the Richmond & Danville Railroad, it was one of the very few railroad construction projects undertaken in the South during the war; it certainly was the most important.

President Jefferson Davis argued that the Danville to Greensboro railroad would "increase greatly the safety and capacity of our means for transporting men and military supplies." It would also considerably cut the time then required for troops and supplies to cross North Carolina. The only rail travel across the state into the Virginia war theater at that time involved use of at least three railroads along circuitous routes, which often took several days.

With most of the men of the South under arms, the problem of securing labor was staggering. Even the 800 hands working on the road by November 10, 1862, was not a sufficient labor force. George W. Randolph, the Confederacy's Secretary of War, wrote to North Carolina's Governor Z.B. Vance on that date pleading for help. Secretary Randolph stressed that "it is considered very important to complete" the railroad and that the Confederate government was doing all it could by supplying at cost such things as rations, tools and horses. But Governor Vance replied that he was powerless to extend any help.

Nevertheless, the builders of the Piedmont Railroad went ahead with such ingenuity and fervor that 1863 actually ended up as a year of accomplishment. By the end of 1863, 600 men were steadily at work on the road, even though they were attracted to the job only by what were called "very high and perhaps extravagant offers of wages."

Grading was completed some seven miles beyond the halfway point at Reidsville, N.C., by the end of the year, and by then, too, track was laid the 28 miles or so from Danville to Reidsville. At the same time, plans were going ahead for laying track northward out of Greensboro.

In September 1863, the 35-ton locomotive *Lee* (bought from the Confederate government) was placed on the road to haul materials for the track crews. In October, a passenger car was attached to the work train and the Piedmont was suddenly a revenue road. In that same month, the 24-ton *Atlas* (bought from the Richmond & Danville) went into service on the road. In November, with boxcars the Piedmont had been able to buy from the R&D, freight service began.

Other purchases of motive power and rolling stock were made that year. From the government, the Piedmont bought the 21-ton *Pettigrew*, the 12-ton *Black Dwarf* and the 18-ton *Roanoke*. From the Richmond & Danville, the 20-ton *Amelia* was purchased.

And it had its rolling stock, too — one first-class coach, two second-class coaches, five boxcars and 20 flatcars, all but six of the cars having been bought from the R&D for $58,000. The remaining six cars were bought from the government.

Confederate and Union raiders during the War made railroads a primary target for destruction. The logs would be set on fire and the rails would bend out of shape by their own weight.
– *Norfolk Southern Corp.*

Before long, however, the Piedmont had its very crucial military usefulness. As the Union came closer to cutting the rail lines running south along the seaboard through Petersburg and Weldon, the Piedmont carried an increasingly heavier military burden. Even before it was completed, it was a principal line of supply for Confederate forces in Virginia.

On May 7, 1864, Colonel A.L. Rives, acting chief of the Confederacy's Engineering Bureau, reported that only four and one-half miles of iron had yet to be laid. On May 22, 1864, the last bar was put in place, and a few days later the first "through-train" passed gingerly along the entire route, a route which Colonel Rives had said in his report was "thoroughly well and intelligently located and constructed."

Floods in January 1865 carried away portions of the track.

But in spite of all, the Piedmont had accomplished some of what it had been built to do. It had helped sustain the Army of Northern Virginia when the other rail lines through Tidewater country had been cut. The railroad proved its military value and that is why it had been built.

Arthur Cochran played a part in the events leading to Georgia's secession. As a member of the Georgia Secession Convention, he joined Alexander H. Stephens (later vice-president of the Confederacy) in opposing Georgia's departure from the Union. But once the issue went against, he loyally supported the Confederacy. During his wartime years as president of the Macon & Brunswick, he remained active in public life. One historian reports that he was a judge during the war.

In 1861 and 1862, the work went slower, although the company's authorized capital had been raised by law to $5 million and the privilege of owning and operating steamships had been granted. (Later the M&B was granted banking privileges as well.)

War, the blockade, and the military needs of the Confederacy took an increasing toll. Iron rail was hardly to be had in the South, and importing it became steadily more difficult as the Union blockade clamped tighter.

In early 1862, the worst flood in 20 years washed out portions of the embankment, track and small bridges along the Ocmulgee River, and the entire track construction force had to concentrate on repairs for several months.

Still, by the end of 1862, the completed track extended for 35 miles out of Macon. Nothing but grading had been done on the southern end of the road near Brunswick. Rolling stock included two locomotives, one passenger car, two baggage and boxcars, and two platform cars. A daily mixed-freight and passenger train made the 70-mile round trip between Macon and Milledgeville Road.

Construction on the uncompleted portion of the line was at a halt, even the grading and line location in the central portion had all been abandoned. Rolling stock was scarce, labor and materials increasingly expensive. One of Cochran's last acts was to save a portion of the completed line from being taken up by the desperate Confederacy.

Cochran did not live to see his railroad reach from Macon to Brunswick. He died in April 1865 at the age of 45. It remained for George Hazlehurst, chief engineer of the road since 1861, to be successor as president and to complete the line in 1871.

Nashville, Tenn., in the 1860s showing destruction of rail equipment along the Nashville and Chattanooga Railroad.
– Norfolk Southern Corp.

In April 1865, the end seemed to be very near, as men in gray watched solemnly as a bearded man stepped from a Richmond & Danville passenger coach in Danville, Va. They formed an honor guard to escort him to a waiting carriage. On April 3, 1865, Jefferson Davis arrived in the city aboard a Richmond & Danville special to carry on his duties as President of the Confederate States of America.

General Grant's stranglehold on the Confederacy's capital in Richmond had forced officials of the Confederate States to leave the city, and as Davis was stepping from the train in Danville, Union troops were entering the Richmond streets. But the one-time United States Secretary of War was not yet ready for surrender. "We will return," he wrote from Danville the day after his arrival. "Let us then not despond, my countrymen, but relying on God, meet the foe with fresh defiance."

Only one chance for "fresh defiance" remained, however; it hung on whether Confederate General Robert E. Lee's Virginia army could join with the forces under General Joseph E. Johnston, then in North Carolina opposing General William T. Sherman. It would be a desperate chance. Grant's and Sherman's men greatly outnumbered the available Confederate troops, but even against these odds of more than five to one, it was still the only alternative to surrender.

The success of this maneuver would depend on using railroads. If Lee could break away at Petersburg and make it past Grant's army to the Richmond & Danville, and if Johnston could move north along the North Carolina and Piedmont railroads, they could join forces at Danville. Doing this would require moving the armies over more than 120 miles of track, through countryside occupied by 180,000 well-supplied Union troops.

On March 19, as Lee prepared to disengage himself from Grant's siege at Richmond and Petersburg, Johnston's army closed with the Federals at Bentonville, N.C., just off the line of the North Carolina Railroad. A furious attack drove the Union forces from their field, but Johnston's men could not pursue and secure their victory until reinforcements arrived the next day. Sherman took advantage of the delay to bring up his entire army, some 80,000 men. Johnston, his own strength only 13,500 men, had no choice but to retreat. Committed to delaying Sherman's advance against the Confederate front, he could do little to stop the Federal cavalry of General George Stoneman that swept down to destroy vital sections of the North Carolina and Piedmont railroads to the Confederate rear.

"This was fatal to the hostile armies of Lee and Johnston," Stoneman later reported, noting that the Confederate forces had depended on the North Carolina and the Piedmont "for supplies and as their ultimate line of retreat."

In Richmond, Lee's food and ammunition were all but gone, his men were starving and growing weaker, and his total force was being reduced in number each day. On April 2, he led the Army of Northern Virginia through Grant's line, heading for the little Virginia town of Amelia Court House, on the Richmond & Danville, where he expected to find supplies.

His plan required critical timing. He had to get ahead of Grant and stay ahead, at the same time managing to feed his army. He had gained a full day on the Union forces when he reached Amelia Court House on April 4. With Grant to his north, he planned to pick up the expected supplies and feed his army on the move southward along the R&D to Danville. But the supplies hadn't arrived, and with his men collapsing from starvation, Lee had no choice but to halt his march and scour the countryside for food. The delay gave Grant's cavalry time to reach the R&D, forcing Lee's men to turn west toward the Virginia village of Appomattox Court House .

On April 7, Grant asked for the surrender of what remained of Lee's army. "Not yet," advised Confederate General James Longstreet when Lee asked for his opinion.

On the morning of April 9, the Army of Northern Virginia passed into history with a last attempt to break through Grant's Union lines, his infantry following close behind. It seemed for a time that Lee's men would succeed, but a steadily growing number of blue-clad troops began closing in from three sides. It was over. Lee surrendered that day — April 9, 1865.

On April 12, President Davis, by this time in Greensboro, N.C., met with members of his cabinet and General Johnston. They had learned that morning of Lee's surrender. There was a division of opinion, but it seemed painfully obvious to most that the cause was lost. The only question was how much more blood would have to be spilled before Johnston, too, would be compelled to yield.

"The members of the Cabinet," General Johnston wrote later, "were then desired by the President to express their opinions on the important question." Johnston was authorized to request an armistice.

The war's first major battle had been on a field near the rail center of Manassas, Va., and now it was coming to an end near the railroad station of Durham, N.C., where General Johnston and General Sherman — their armies facing one another down the line of the battered North Carolina Rail Road — met to conclude the terms of surrender. On April 26, 1865, the last major Confederate army agreed to lay down its arms.

The world's first "Railroad War" was over!

The war would continue for a few more months in some of the Western Territories, but in the South the guns fell silent.

The glory and the grandeur of the prewar South was now gone forever. As far as the eye could see, there was only destruction. The railroads that were the pride of the South before the war now lay in ruins, but they, like the South, would rise from the ashes to become even greater.

Draped in black and accompanied by the military escort, this car carried the body of President Abraham Lincoln from Washington to Springfield, Ill., in 1865. The car was intended for the use of the President, but he never rode in it during his lifetime and its one official use was to carry his body to Springfield.

- Norfolk Southern Corp.

Chapter III

Reconstruction
1866 – 1870

For four years the South's railroads had been fought over, run into the ground, wrecked, rebuilt and wrecked again. Some had been destroyed outright, while others had been torn up so that the rails as well as the locomotives and cars could be used for a greater military advantage.

At war's end, most of the South's railroads were in the possession of the Union forces, and getting them back from the Federal government proved to be quite a problem for their owners. Most of the vanished rolling stock was now gone forever.

But like a phoenix, the South's railroads rose from their own ashes. Railroad men recovered and rebuilt the battered lines. Often they combined them into larger and stronger systems to help bring to life again a region that lay in ruins.

It was all that the South could do to rebuild its railroads and construct the new rail links that were absolutely necessary to the region's development. But the South had neither the means nor the incentive for the kind of railroad-building that took place in the victorious North.

So the South emerged at the turn of the century with a lean, strong railway system without the excess trackage that was to later plague the railroads of the Northeast and Midwest.

The Civil War had left deep scars on the railroads that were to become the Southern Railway. Throughout the South, tracks, buildings and equipment had been destroyed. The Orange & Alexandria's facilities at Alexandria and its line south had been commandeered and used by the Union army. Its Alexandria shops had become the military car shops of the Union army, where, in 1864 and 1865, a special car had been constructed for the intended use of President Lincoln.

After 1865, the South's railroads battled for survival amidst wrecked facilities and equipment, and the virtual worthlessness of the Confederate bonds and currency they held. Consolidation helped to save many of them.

For example, logic pointed to a postwar combination of the two lines extending north and south from Knoxville. In 1869, the line from Dalton, Ga., to Bristol, Va., was consolidated as the East Tennessee, Virginia & Georgia Railroad Company. During the period 1872-1890, the ETV&G would extend its interests to other rail lines in North Carolina, Alabama, Georgia and Kentucky.

Principally, the ETV&G acquired control of the Memphis & Charleston; the Selma, Rome & Dalton Railroad (running from Selma, Ala., to Dalton, Ga.); the Cincinnati Southern Railway (extending from Cincinnati, Ohio, to Chattanooga, Tenn.); and the Alabama Great Southern Railway (Chattanooga to Meridian, Miss.).

The latter two lines are of particular interest. The Cincinnati Southern had been built by the City of Cincinnati to offset the trading advantage enjoyed by Louisville, Ky., as a result of the Louisville & Nashville Railroad. Authorized in 1869, construction began in 1873. It was completed in 1880 and was leased in 1881 for operation by the Cincinnati, New Orleans & Texas Pacific Railway. The successful bidders who obtained the lease and organized the CNO&TP to operate the line from Cincinnati to Chattanooga also gained control of a connecting line from there to Meridian, Miss.

This line began at each end and worked toward the middle. The Wills Valley Railroad, chartered in 1852, by 1860 had constructed some 12 miles of railroad from Wauhatchie southeast to Trenton, Ga. Meanwhile, the Northeast & Southwest Alabama Railroad, chartered in 1853, had built a line of road northeast from Meridian to York, Ala. A proposal to consolidate the two lines was interrupted by the war, but was put into effect in 1868 when the two were joined as the Alabama & Chattanooga Railroad. Construction of the line was completed by 1871, and the company thereafter went into receivership and was sold to the English investors of Messrs. Emile Erlanger & Co., who reorganized it as the Alabama Great Southern Railway Company.

War's end found the East Tennessee & Georgia fairly intact, although an inventory report from the state road commissioner to the Tennessee General Assembly said the road "met with its full share of the calamities of the war." The commissioner estimated the ET&G's wartime losses from property destroyed or damaged at more than $375,000.

This gloomy report was partially offset by the road's discovery that the wartime shuffling of rolling stock and motive power between the South's railroads had ended in the ET&G's favor. The road had wound up with one more locomotive than it had when the war began and almost as many cars. But, as later events proved, this expected bonanza turned out to be costly in other ways.

Added to the primary problem of rebuilding, another worry facing the road's owners was the accumulation of interest due the road's bondholders, who had not been paid during the war. This amounted to about $275,000, more than half of it owed to the State of Tennessee.

To protect their interests, and while the road was still occupied by the Union army, a group of ET&G stockholders met in July 1865 and appointed a president to manage the company's affairs until a formal election could be held. The selection fell on Thomas Callaway, a native Tennesseean whose parents had migrated from North Carolina.

Callaway's appointment was his second experience as head of the road. He had served as the ET&G's second president during 1852-53, but had resigned to devote his time to other interests, though he continued to serve as a director in the ensuing years. He was to serve briefly as president of the connecting road to the north, the East Tennessee & Virginia, and as first president of the combined companies when they merged a few years later as the East Tennessee, Virginia & Georgia.

Shortly after Callaway assumed office, U.S. Secretary of War Edwin M. Staton directed the military authorities in Tennessee to return all railroads to their owners. Callaway took possession of the East Tennessee & Georgia on August 28, 1865, receiving it from General George H. Thomas, who commanded the Department of the Cumberland in Tennessee.

This apparent leniency by the War Department had one significant string attached. Rather than attempt to sort out and return the widely scattered equipment to its owner roads, the Federal government exercised the right of a victor to dispose of captured enemy property on its own terms. It offered to sell to the ET&G whatever equipment the road felt it needed that hadn't originally belonged to it.

Thomas Callaway agreed to buy much of the foreign equipment the road had found on its line. But, as he later explained, he did so under protest and only because he had no choice if the road was to have enough locomotives and cars. He felt that the government owed his railroad a sum greater than the purchase price for the Union army's use of the road during the war and for damages the Northern troops inflicted on the road's property. In support of this claim, he argued that when the road had been turned over to Northern General Burnside in the fall of 1863, the military commander had agreed to reimburse the road for its use by his army.

Nevertheless, to obtain the equipment, Callaway had to sign a bond for $371,000. This amount, which he considered far more than the equipment was worth, was to be paid by the railway in 24 monthly installments, along with interest set by the government at $7\frac{3}{10}$ percent annually.

By June 1866, the ET&G had reduced this debt some $40,000 through transportation and mail service furnished to the government. Rebuilding of the damaged track had begun and arrangements were being made to pay off the accumulated interest to the state.

The following year, however, the company's finances were spread so thinly that the road began to fall behind on its payments to the government. This brought a curt reminder from the Department of the Cumberland. " . . . You are expected to pay every cent your Company can appropriate to the liquidation of this debt at once," said the letter to Callaway dated August 15, 1867, "and provide definitely for the payment becoming due in the future. If you are not heard from by the 28th, I shall proceed to enforce the terms of your Bond. Immediate action in this matter is requested." The letter was signed "By Command of Maj. Gen. Thomas." Despite the letter's emphatic tones, Callaway asked for an extension on the payments and pleaded his company's poor finances. He was turned down.

Callaway then began his own offensive. He presented a counterclaim to the U.S. government for a precise $632,066.38. This, he said, was the amount due the ET&G for war damages and for the Union army's use of the road during the war. Furthermore, the rail president added, the State of Tennessee had a prior claim on the company's earnings as a result of the state's ownership of a majority of the road's stock. He explained to the War Department that the "scanty" revenues of the company were being applied to a payment of interest on the state mortgage to prevent foreclosure.

This diamond-stacked steam locomotive of the days when the Central of Georgia was known as the Central Railroad & Banking Company of Georgia.

- Norfolk Southern Corp.

This approach apparently won an extension for payments until the first of the following year (1868). By that April, however, the ET&G was still resisting the efforts of the War Department to collect not only the monthly payments, but also an accumulation of interest amounting to some $9,000.

From Washington, the Quartermaster General of the U.S., J.J. Dana, took a hand in the game. In a letter to Callaway on April 10, 1868, Dana said no further extension could be granted. And, in reply to the rail president's counterclaim against the government, he added a grim reminder that the road was considered to be captured enemy property and the government, therefore, owed nothing for its use during the war. The letter also pointed out that the government didn't recognize any prior claims on the company's earnings, including that of the State of Tennessee.

Meanwhile, a prewar plan to merge the East Tennessee & Georgia with its northern rail neighbor, the East Tennessee & Virginia, was being revived. A firm step in this direction was taken by the stockholders of the ET&V on the death of their president, John R. Branner, in February 1869, when they elected Callaway as his successor. Callaway at the same time was president of the ET&G.

As the two railroads together had contracted a total of $625,000 in debts to the government for equipment purchased after the war, the War Department was able to direct its demand for payment to a single source, Thomas H. Callaway. But it was no more successful at collecting the joint debt than it was when dealing with the two roads individually. Consequently, in August 1869, the Quartermaster General, then M.C. Meigs, informed Callaway that he had appointed a receiver to take over the two companies and cited nonpayment of debts as the reason. He ordered that the property of the railroads be turned over to the receiver "without delay."

Callaway received this letter, along with one written by the appointed receiver, on August 23 and promptly replied to both. Stating that he had no authority to comply with the request, he "respectfully declined" to release control of the two roads and, in turn, challenged the legal right of the U.S. to seize the roads.

This stubborn refusal apparently achieved a stalemate between Callaway and the government. No other reference to the litigation appears in the two companies' records until the second annual report of the East Tennessee, Virginia & Georgia Railroad Company (the consolidation of the two roads took effect on November 26, 1869) dated 1871. It mentioned that "Congress . . . at its last session passed a law empowering the Secretary of War to compromise and adjust litigation between the United States and the sundry railroads . . . ."

Final settlement between the railroads and the U.S. on the drawn-out controversy came in May 1872. Of the total debt claimed by the government, $625,000 minus small sums collected from the two roads, the ETV&G paid $5,000 in cash and signed notes of 10 and 15 years for another total of $190,000.

Callaway's cold war with the Union had ended, but the militant Tennessean did not live to see even this partial victory. He died on August 29, 1870, at the age of 58, less than a year after he became the first president of the East Tennessee, Virginia & Georgia Railroad.

The ETV&G expanded into one of the great railway systems of the South, before going bankrupt. The line was sold to the Southern Railway Company in 1894. In a large measure, however, the East Tennessee, Virginia & Georgia owed its existence to Thomas Howard Callaway, who fought the War Department to a standstill and preserved the private ownership of the roads placed in his charge.

Another company that had its share of problems was the Orange & Alexandria. War's end in 1865 was to be the end of one set of difficulties and the beginning of another for the O&A. By the early part of 1866, President Barbour had negotiated the return of the line to its owners. But they faced a massive task of rebuilding. Many station buildings had been burned out and never replaced. Repairs to track and bridges by the military had been done principally to get trains through, rather than to build substantially for future operations and maintenance.

War's end found the Manassas Gap Railroad, which connected the O&A at Manassas with the fertile Shenandoah Valley, in even worse straits. Most of its rails and rolling stock had been carried away for use elsewhere in response to the demands of the military.

Stockholders of both companies agreed to, and the state legislature authorized, a merger of the two companies in 1867 as the Orange, Alexandria & Manassas Railroad Company. John S. Barbour was unanimously elected to head the new company.

His drive to build and extend the road immediately became apparent. In addition to the rebuilding of both roads and the extension of the Manassas Gap to Harrisonburg, the new company undertook to aid a newly formed company (the Lynchburg & Danville Railroad Company) in building a line from Lynchburg to Danville, Va. (now Southern's main line). Before the line to Harrisonburg (1873) or the Danville extensions were completed (1874), the three companies became one — the Washington City, Virginia Midland & Great Southern — still under the leadership of John S. Barbour.

When heavy prewar debt and the commercial depression of the area drove the company into receivership, John S. Barbour became the receiver of the property. He was still at its head when the company emerged in 1881 as the Virginia Midland Railway Company.

The Charlotte & South Carolina Railway Company had to be totally rebuilt in 1865, but it was still able to extend generous aid during the reconstruction period to connecting lines such as the Atlantic, Tennessee & Ohio, in which the C&S became a large stockholder; the King's Mountain Railroad, which was engaged in the construction of a narrow-gauge line from Chester, S.C., and which was operated afterwards by the Charlotte, Columbia & Augusta under the name of Chester & Lenoir Railroad; and finally to the Columbia & Augusta Railroad, which it ended up absorbing.

The Charlotte & South Carolina Railroad was a majority stockholder in the Columbia & Augusta Railroad, and the interests of the two companies were the same. A proposition was set in motion in 1868 for their consolidation, and in 1869 authority was obtained from the states of Georgia, South and North Carolina in three acts, all of which provided: "The Charlotte and South Carolina Railroad Company and the Columbia and Augusta Railroad Company shall upon consent of the stockholders of each company be consolidated and form one and the same body corporate under the name of the Charlotte, Columbia and Augusta Railroad Company, possessing all the rights, powers, privileges, immunities and franchises conferred upon said companies by the several Acts heretofore passed and now in force incorporating said companies and amending the charters thereof."

In 1868, the Louisville, Harrodsburg & Virginia Railroad Company was incorporated in Kentucky to construct a railroad line from Louisville to the Kentucky and Virginia state lines in the direction of Wytheville, Va.

President Tate of the Memphis & Charleston Railroad said at a special meeting of the stockholders in July 1865: "I went to Washington and presented the organization to the President, who approved it, and on the 8th of August gave an order to the military commander of the Division of the Tennessee to have the Road and property belonging to it turned over to the Company."

On September 3, the eastern division, Stevenson to Decatur, was released by the military. Eight days later, the western division, Memphis to Pocahontas, was returned to its owners.

The gap from Pocahontas to Decatur, 114 miles, was, in the words of Tate, "almost entirely destroyed, except the Road bed and iron rails, and they were in very bad condition — every bridge and trestle destroyed, cross-ties rotten, buildings burned, water tanks gone, ditches filled up, and track grown up in weeds and bushes; and not a saw-mill near the line, and the labor system of the country gone.

"About 40 miles of the track was burned, cross-ties entirely destroyed, and rails bent and twisted in such manner as to require great labor to straighten and a large portion of them requiring renewal.

"What little machinery you had left was principally scattered over the South and cut off from you, and had been run for four years with little or no repairs."

That was the gloomy prospect facing the Memphis & Charleston in 1865. Practically all equipment needed heavy repairs, which the company was in no condition to make. More than 100 miles of road had to be rebuilt completely. All buildings had to be renewed. In all, the company had nearly 300 miles of road to equip and run with little cash and even less credit.

Like the rest of the South, the M&C somehow managed to rise from its own ashes. Under the terms of the presidential order, the railroad purchased from the military on credit 10 locomotives, 226 freight cars, 14 passenger cars, a number of shop tools and a supply of road and shop materials. The expense came to almost a half-million dollars, for which the government received the company's bond and the personal security of its officers that the debt would be paid in two years, either in cash or in transportation service.

In addition, the government turned over to the M&C 18 locomotives captured early in the war, 10 of them in reasonably good condition. As fast as the track could be put in order, trains began to run over the line. By November 6, 1865, the line was completely open save for the 1,700-foot bridge destroyed at Decatur. (Passengers and freight were transferred by steamer at that point.) By July 1866, a new and better bridge was completed.

"Your trains are now running through (to Chattanooga)," Tate told the stockholders at that time, "with close connections to New York and all points on the Atlantic coast, and arrangements are in progress by which a fast freight line will be put in on the line to New York, Norfolk, Charleston and Savannah . . . by which it is believed that your business will be greatly increased."

Reconstruction in the South was well under way, but for the railroads, the times were changing. The rebuilding for the most part was over; now it was time for the railroads to expand, either by building or by consolidation. The country was reunited and the move west was on, opening up new territories that would in a few years become the western states. But in the South, the railroads were about to face their next biggest challenge.

Charleston, Cincinnati & Chicago RR., No. 1. A 4-4-0 type, named *Gov. Senter*. Later this engine was on the R&D, and then on the Southern.
— *Collection of Fred W. Bruce*

Chapter IV

Transition
1871 – 1893

On November 18, 1868, the first two predecessor lines of the Alabama Great Southern, the North East & South West Alabama and the Wills Valley, were consolidated to form the Alabama & Chattanooga Railroad. It became Birmingham's first railroad.

Physically, the Alabama & Chattanooga then consisted of 27 miles of line, from Meridian to York, and 12 miles of line between Wauhatchie and Trenton. To join the two lines required about 250 miles of railroad, which was finally completed on May 17, 1871. There is no record available of the exact date that the line was constructed through Elyton, but it must have been between April 10, 1869, and May 17, 1871, probably sometime in the latter part of 1870.

Financial difficulties beset the A&C from the beginning, the road defaulting in the payment of interest on its bonds on January 1, 1871. In March of the same year, the governor of Alabama seized the road's property in Alabama, Mississippi and Tennessee, while the governor of Georgia similarly seized the road's property in his state. More than seven years of litigation followed, ending in the purchase of the property by Emile Erlanger & Company, an English banking concern, in June 1877. The name of the road was then changed to the Alabama Great Southern Railroad.

Rehabilitation of the line started soon after, and the beginnings of what is now Southern Railway System in Alabama can be seen in the Erlanger acquisition of controlling interests in the New Orleans & Northeastern Railroad (extending from Meridian to New Orleans), the Cincinnati, New Orleans & Texas Pacific Railroad (extending from Cincinnati to Chattanooga), and a number of other lines in Mississippi and Louisiana. It was during this period of English ownership that the popular "Queen and Crescent Route" was set up.

In the post-Civil War period, the Richmond & Danville was also busy expanding its railway system. It obtained control of the North Carolina in 1871 and the Northwestern North Carolina Railroad (Greensboro to Salem) in 1872. The Charlotte, Columbia & Augusta came in the R&D system in 1878, and three years later the R&D took possession of the Atlanta & Charlotte Air Line Railway with its branch lines. The expansion continued to take in other small lines in Virginia and North Carolina.

The East Tennessee, Virginia & Georgia and the Richmond & Danville, both directed by the Richmond Terminal Company, purchased control of the Alabama Great Southern and the Cincinnati, New Orleans & Texas Pacific in 1890, further expanding the two systems. The Richmond Terminal Company had already obtained control of the Virginia Midland Railway Company (the old Orange, Alexandria and Manassas line from Alexandria south) and that line had become officially part of the Richmond & Danville in 1886.

On April 28, 1884, an act was approved to change the name of the Louisville, Harrodsburg & Virginia Railroad Company to the Louisville Southern Railroad Company. In 1887, the construction began on a proposed line from Louisville to a connection with the Cincinnati Southern Railway at Danville, Ky., eight miles north of Danville, where it linked with the Cincinnati Southern.

On May 30, 1888, the Louisville Southern officially opened the track.

On December 10, 1888, the Louisville Southern Railroad leased its property, including the line from Louisville to Burgin, to the Louisville, New Albany & Chicago Railway Company. The line was operated as part of this system until March 27, 1890, when the lease was abrogated by mutual consent.

While the Louisville Southern was part of this system, it wanted to build branches from Lawrenceburg to Lexington and Georgetown to connect with Louisville & Nashville, Chesapeake & Ohio, and the Kentucky Midland railroads, and the Cincinnati Southern Railway. In order to complete the line, a bridge was needed to cross the Kentucky River. On October 9, 1888, Congress approved the plan to build a bridge at Youngs High Bridge, Ky., connecting Lawrenceburg to Lexington through Tyrone and Versaille. The bridge was constructed in 1888 and the line was completed on August 24, 1889.

In the spring of 1890, the East Tennessee system wanted to gain an entrance to the Louisville market, and so the East Tennessee, Virginia & Georgia Railway leased the Louisville Southern. The East Tennessee subsequently bought controlling interest in the Louisville Southern.

The ETV&G receivers assumed the operation of the Louisville Southern until 1893, when separate receivers of the Louisville Southern were appointed and operated the line until a reorganization was effected. This reorganization consolidated the various properties of the line and the title was vested in the name of the Southern Railway Company, the Kentucky corporation which had been organized by the purchasers of the Richmond & Danville Railroad. This began the operation of the Southern Railway System in Kentucky.

"If there are men who can accomplish results better and faster under similar difficulties, in the name of Heaven bring them to the work." General Nathan Forrest, first president of the Selma, Marion & Memphis Railroad Company, expressed himself forcefully, as was his usual way when his opinion was needed. In describing to the stockholders, in February 1872, the problems they faced in trying to build a 280-mile railroad through a war-ravaged land, he was as blunt and direct as ever. Forrest, one of the Confederacy's finest fighting men, was engaged in another great struggle on behalf of the South, the effort to build a railroad from Memphis, Tenn., to Selma, Ala.

A tight money market, forerunner of the full-scale financial panic of 1873, made it difficult to raise money for the road's construction through the sale of mortgage bonds. The recent failure of another Alabama railroad to meet the interest on its bonds did nothing to reassure investors. Payments on individual stock subscriptions, and on those voted by various counties along the proposed route, were slow to come in. In one county, legal action had been started to block the payment of the county's subscription. Failure of the cotton crop reduced revenues on the small portion of the line already completed. Hopes for a line from Memphis into the potentially cotton- and mineral-rich areas of Northern Alabama were in part based on the charters and 13 miles of track that were all that was left of the attempts by a succession of small companies to build a railroad across Northern Alabama before the war.

In 1868 and early 1869, two companies were formed to further this plan. The intent now was to build toward Memphis rather than toward Montgomery, Ala., which had been the earlier plan. Both of the companies were named the Selma, Marion & Memphis Railroad, and Nathan Bedford Forrest headed them both. One was chartered in Alabama to assume the franchise and properties of the Cahaba, Marion & Greensboro Railroad, which owned 13 miles of line between Marion and Marion Junction, Ala., completed in 1856. The other, chartered in Mississippi and Tennessee, took over the charter of Memphis, Holly Springs, Okolona & Selma Railroad, which had no tracks laid.

Nathan Bedford Forrest, noted Confederate General who became first president of the Selma, Marion & Memphis Railroad Co. after the Civil War.

– Norfolk Southern Corp.

For more than four years, Forrest devoted all his energies to the struggle to get his railroad into existence. He was instrumental in obtaining support for the $500,000 stock subscription voted by the people of Memphis and Shelby County. He and the men who worked with him canvassed the eight counties in Mississippi and five in Alabama through which the railroad would run, speaking to the railroad conventions and meetings of citizens. In some counties, Forrest spoke in every civil district.

Though the two companies joined forces in 1871, the difficulties still proved too great. Forrest's trips to New York to spur the sale of the road's bonds helped little. In the attempt to get the road built, he used the company's means and his own as strategically as he had once employed his men in battle. Yet only 50 miles of line were completed during his years as president (he resigned in 1874).

This 4-4-0 American-type locomotive poses for its picture back in 1880.   – *Author's collection.*

The road went bankrupt and was never fully extended as planned. But sections of the road became part of two major U.S. railroads, one section being the Southern's line from Marion Junction to Akron, Ala. In that way, the railroad eventually contributed to the South's progress, as Forrest intended that it should. He believed in railroads and the future of Memphis as a railroad center. What he believed in, he fought for. To lay to Forrest's account the failure of the Selma, Marion & Memphis is to ignore the financial difficulties the builders faced, the impoverished condition of the region and the measure of the men.

The Cincinnati Southern began work at the south portal of King's Mountain tunnel on December 23, 1873, and the road was completed from Ludlow to Somerset on July 23, 1877, when the first passenger train was operated. The first freight train was operated as far as Somerset on August 13, 1877. The line was completed through to Chattanooga on December 10, 1879, and the first freight train through to Chattanooga was operated on March 8, 1880. This was a great occasion for Cincinnati and was climaxed by a banquet in the Music Hall on March 17, 1880. It was attended by more than 1,700 people prominent in public and business life, many of them coming from the South in excursion trains operated by the new railroad.

Originally, the road had 27 tunnels and 105 bridges and viaducts, including four large spans over the Ohio, Kentucky, Cumberland and Tennessee rivers. The span over the Kentucky River known as the "High Bridge" is more than 300 feet above the water and was the first "cantilever" built in America. The Ohio River bridge contained the longest "truss" span built up to that time. Many of the tunnels have since been eliminated.

The original gauge was 5 feet, with rail of 53 to 60 pounds per yard. On Sunday, May 30, 1886, it was changed to the standard gauge of 4 feet 8½ inches, and the work was completed in 13 hours at a cost of $23,396.97. The cost of changing the rolling stock was $31,007.02. This made it possible to interchange equipment with connections and saved the heavy expense and delay of transferring freight, particularly at Cincinnati. (At present, about 75 percent of the line is double-track, with rail ranging to 140 pounds per yard.)

On March 11, 1881, the General Assembly of Ohio passed an act directing the trustees to sell or lease the road (Cincinnati Southern) on terms and conditions to be fixed by the trustees. On September 7, 1881, a company known as the Cincinnati, New Orleans & Texas Pacific Railway Company was organized to lease the road. The lease was negotiated with the trustees for a period of 25 years from October 12, 1881.

The first president of the Cincinnati, New Orleans & Texas Pacific Railway was Theodore Cook, a prominent citizen of Ohio, who served from October 1881 to December 1882. He was succeeded by John Scott, an Englishman with many years of railroad experience. Scott was also president of the Alabama Great Southern, New Orleans & North Eastern, Alabama & Vicksburg, and Vicksburg, Shreveport & Pacific railroads. Scott resigned on January 1, 1885, and was succeeded by Frank S. Bond, who served until December 23, 1886, when he resigned to accept the vice-presidency of the Chicago, Milwaukee & St. Paul Railway Company. Charles Schiff was elected president, serving until November 7, 1890, when he was succeeded by Samuel M. Felton. Felton was only 37 years old when he came to the CNO&TP. He had been with the CNO&TP for about three years when he was named receiver by Judge William H. Taft of the U.S. Circuit Court of the Southern District of Ohio. The receivership was terminated after six and one-half years, on September 30, 1899, when the line passed to the control of the Southern Railway. On October 16, 1899, Samuel Spencer was made president. At that time Felton resigned and was elected to the presidency of the Alton Railroad.

On March 12, 1887, the Ohio legislature passed a bill authorizing the sale of the road, subject to approval by a majority vote of the people of Cincinnati. No offer was made the city, however, until June 13, 1896, when a joint offer was made by the Southern Railway and the Cincinnati, Hamilton & Dayton Railroad. But at a special election held on August 3, 1896, the offer was rejected by a small margin.

The grading of the Chester & Lenoir Narrow Gauge Railroad was formally begun on Friday, March 27, 1874, at two o'clock p.m. on the Harper and Beall contract near Lenoir, N.C.

According to the charters granted by the states of North and South Carolina, the Carolina Narrow Gauge was consolidated with the Chester & Lenoir Narrow Gauge Company on May 14, 1873, at Hickory, N.C. On April 3, 1874, the final act was adopted authorizing the purchase and consolidation of the King's Mountain Railroad Company with the Chester & Lenoir Company. This road had a broad gauge and ran from Chester to Yorkville, a distance of 27 miles. The Chester & Lenoir Company paid $85,000 for it and got the iron, all the rolling stock and $8,004.90 in cash assets. Consolidation of the companies thus being effected, the road now ran from Chester to Lenoir via Yorkville, Dallas, Lincolnton, Newton, and Hickory, a distance of 110 miles.

In August 1878, the Caldwell contracting company was formed, and with convict labor this company completed the grading from Lenoir to Hickory in May 1879, at a cost of $14,000. The piers of the bridge over the Catawaba River were also built with convict labor. They cost $4,500. With the grading completed — except between Newton and Hickory — and the piers of the Catawaba bridge built, the company was still lacking the means to purchase the iron and cross-ties.

After considering various propositions, the stockholders agreed to lease the road to the Charlotte, Columbia & Augusta Railroad. This lease was made in September 1882 and required the completion of the road to Newton by July 1, 1883, and to Lenoir by March 22, 1884. This company began laying track at Maiden, seven miles below Newton, on time. Then an arrangement was made with the Western North Carolina Railroad to lay a third rail on their track to Hickory, which was reached sometime in January 1884. Captain Waddill, with a large force, began at once to lay the track, but the work was severely hampered by rain and snow, ice and mud. It was found impossible to reach Lenoir by March 22. The stockholders met at Dallas, N.C., on March 23 and extended the deadline to June 1.

The Catawaba bridge was finished on February 7, and the same day the first locomotive entered Caldwell. Mr. Azor Shell, who had the contract for building all the trestles between Hickory and Lenoir, finished the Lower Creek trestle on Wednesday, May 14, and on Saturday, May 17, the first train entered Lenoir.

When the first train entered the Lenoir corporate limits in May 1884, the surrounding country still abounded in wild game and trails were about the only avenues of travel. The population of the town was then

CNO&TP compound No. 604, a 4-6-0-type built by Baldwin in 1889.   – *Collection of Fred W. Bruce.*

only about 300 or 400 people. Think what a train would have meant. For ten years, the grading and construction work had been under way, and when a freight train finally reached there on the night of May 17, a dream was realized.

The completion of the road was marked by a celebration on June 5, 1884. It was attended by representatives from Chester, Gaston, Lincoln and Catawaba counties, as well as from counties to the north, east and west. The last spike in the railroad track, a gold one, was set in place by Mr. Haskell, president of the road, and was driven in by Colonel Green Moore, one of the three men who had shoveled the dirt at the start of grading ten years before. He was the only one of the three to live to see the road completed.

Forty-four years later, in 1928, the Carolina & Northwestern Railroad extended the road from Chester, S.C., to Edgemont, N.C., making it the main artery of transportation for this section of state. Built as a narrow-gauge railroad to Lenoir in 1884, it was later converted to a broad-gauge and extended to Edgemont. It was known as the Chester & Lenoir Railroad, but was later changed to the Carolina & Northwestern.

A tall, graying, handsome Virginian faced the crowd in the Virginia Midland offices at Alexandria, on a March Saturday in 1885. In his hands, he cradled a magnificent gold watch, a parting gift from the men he had led for more than three decades. Behind small, gold-rimmed spectacles, his eyes grew a little misty as one of them read from an illuminated booklet: "The employees of the Virginia Midland Railway Company, of every rank and condition, with one voice and by common consent, thus unite to express their hearty good will toward the Honorable John S. Barbour, Jr., and in fitting words to tell their sorrow that he resigned the office of president of their roads . . . ."

Louisville Southern engine No. 2, 4-4-0 train 11 on Ox Trestle near Lawrenceburg, Ky., 1892.

- Collection of Fred W. Bruce.

John S. Barbour, Jr., lawyer, legislator and railroad president, was leaving what he considered the great work of his life, leadership of the rail line that ran southward and westward from Alexandria through the heart of Virginia. Extending more than 400 miles, including branch lines, and already combined with the strong Richmond & Danville Railroad System, the Virginia Midland had outgrown its need for the sure hand that had kept it growing through the war, uneasy peace and financial difficulties.

A few months before, John Barbour had declined nomination for a thirty-fourth year at the head of the company, though he did intend to remain as a director as long as the stockholders wanted him. Now he could devote more time to the demanding job of representing his district of Virginia in the U.S. House of Representatives.

"In the infancy of the company he was placed at its head and controlled its destinies for over 34 years. He found it scarcely reaching beyond the corporate limits of Alexandria, waging a doubtful struggle for existence. He left it with 411 miles of completed railway, spanning the state and vitalizing its midland belt . . . ."

Nor did he lose touch with railroading. He continued as a director to the Virginia Midland, and in 1887 became its vice-president as well. From 1888 until his death in 1892, he was director of the Richmond & Danville Railroad. He did not live to see the Virginia Midland and the Richmond & Danville become a part of the vast rail network of the Southern Railway. But his calm judgement, common sense and tact, and his faculty for inspiring courage and confidence helped bring the Orange & Alexandria through war and depression to its present place as a vital link in the Southern Railway System.

Chapter V

Southern Railway
1894 – 1982

Thus the stage was set for the Southern Railway System. Organized on July 1, 1894, it contained only the central southeastern framework of today's Southern. Basically, it was a combination of the Richmond & Danville system and the East Tennessee, Virginia & Georgia. Two-thirds of the approximately 4,400 miles of line the company operated was owned outright. The rest was held through leases, operating agreements and stock ownership.

In addition, Southern controlled lines like the Alabama Great Southern and the Georgia Southern & Florida, although they were separately operated. It also had less than a controlling interest in other lines, like the Central of Georgia.

The first stage of Southern's growth involved two major efforts: making the core system operate efficiently and profitably, and bringing into closer coordination the separately operated lines. Samuel Spencer, the railway's first president, was well suited to both tasks. Widely experienced in railroad operations and financing, he had been one of the architects of the plan to reorganize the sprawling R&D system. He knew the value of reshaping its loose confederation of independently operated companies into a tightly knit, centrally controlled rail network.

During Samuel Spencer's 12 years as president, Southern's pattern of growth began to emerge. Other lines were drawn into Southern's core system. New shops were built at Knoxville, Tenn., and Atlanta. Year by year, locomotives and cars were added to a growing equipment fleet.

Southern moved quickly to develop its territory and has continued to do so for more than 90 years in response to the South's changing needs.

Geographical expansion and improvement of the physical plant continued in two successive presidencies, those of William F. Finley (1906-1913) and Fairfax Harrison (1914-1937). By the time the line from Meridian, Miss., to New Orleans was acquired in 1916, Southern had attained the 8,000-mile, 13-state system that was to mark the limit of its territorial expansion for almost half a century.

The important line from Cincinnati to Chattanooga, completed in 1880, was built and is owned by the City of Cincinnati. It is leased by the city to the Cincinnati, New Orleans & Texas Pacific Railway Company. The CNO&TP is controlled by the Southern Railway through stock ownership. Since 1917, it has been operated as part of the Southern Railway System.

In 1901, the Louisville, Evansville & St. Louis Consolidated Railroad became a part of the Southern.

Steam was to know its greatest years on the Southern in the 1920s and 1930s, when Mikados, Mountains, and green and gold Pacifics ranged the network of rails at the head of some of the South's finest freight and passenger trains.

On a quiet, peaceful Sunday afternoon in 1903, a southbound mail train was running an hour late, but she was right on time for her appointment with destiny. At 3 p.m. on September 27, 1903, her whistle screamed farewell to the world, and in doing so took the lives of 11 men and injured seven others. She also left her mark on the pages of American history. Recorded is the following: Engineer Joseph A. Broady, Engine Number 1102, Mail Run 97, Stillhouse Trestle.

Number 97 operated between New York and New Orleans and was the fastest train on the Virginia Midland branch of the Southern Railway. On that fateful Sunday, it wrecked just outside of the Danville yard limits. The train left the track just as it was entering a high trestle on the steep grade and curve that spans

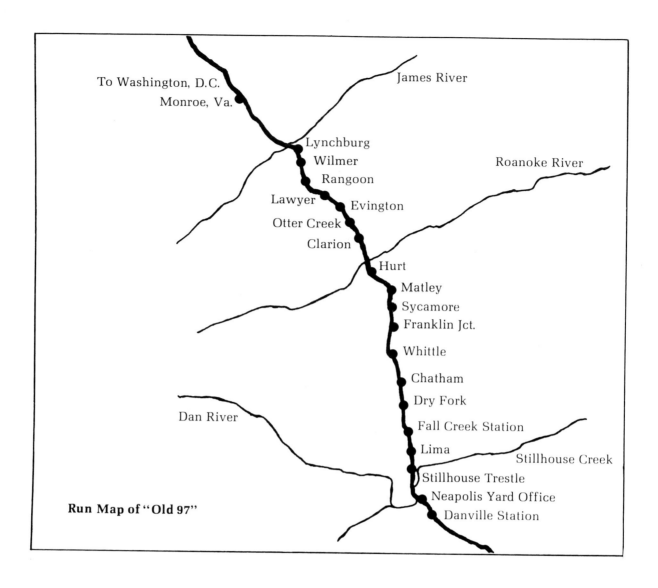

To Washington, D.C.
Monroe, Va.
James River

Lynchburg
Wilmer
Rangoon
Roanoke River

Lawyer
Evington
Otter Creek
Clarion

Hurt
Matley
Sycamore
Franklin Jct.

Whittle

Chatham
Dry Fork

Dan River
Fall Creek Station

Lima
Stillhouse Creek

Stillhouse Trestle
Neapolis Yard Office
Danville Station

Run Map of "Old 97"

Stillhouse Creek. It was presumed — definite information being unavailable on account of the death of the engineer and conductor — that the train had been running at an unusually high rate of speed, and that the flange on a wheel of the engine had broken when it struck the curve. The engine, pushed by two mail cars, one baggage and one express car, ran some distance on the trestle, plunging along the cross-ties, and then fell 75 feet to the water below.

Of the men who composed the train crew, 11 were killed and seven were seriously injured. Engineer J. A. Broady of Saltville, Va., stuck to his post, but was thrown some distance from the engine. He was found dead, lying in the water of the creek. Conductor J. Thomas Blair of Spencer, N.C., was also killed. His body was among the first to be recovered from the wreck.

The scene of the wreck defied description, as all of the coaches were piled upon each other. The engine itself was buried in the mud at the bottom of the creek, with the debris of the wreckage scattered over the area. The telegraph wires that were running parallel with the track were torn down and communications were delayed.

It was said that the engineer of the doomed train had only been running a fast mail for a short time. Number 97 was the fastest train on the road. People living in the vicinity along either side of the tracks, many of whom were eyewitnesses to the disaster, said they were appalled at the rate of speed at which the train was running.

Vice-president Finley of the Southern Railway was interviewed the following morning (September 28, 1903) regarding the accident, and said, "The train consisted of two postal cars, one express car and one baggage car for the storage of the mail. The trestle was damaged very little, as the train jumped the track about 40 feet

48

This photo was taken about one hour after the wreck of Old 97. Photo is looking west across the wreckage with Stillhouse Trestle in the background.

- *Author's collection.*

This photo is looking east at the wreck. Here rails and other debris can be seen in foreground. Notice that smoke and steam are clouding the view.

- Norfolk Southern Corp.

Monday morning work begins anew to look for the other bodies. The workmen worked all through the night looking for the missing.

– Norfolk Southern Corp.

north of the trestle on sound track in good line and surface and proper gauge. The trestle was in first-class condition, and was so well braced that the engine and train, falling on the outside of the curve, knocked down only the outside post, but left the other side standing. Eyewitnesses report that the train was approaching the trestle at a rate of speed of 30 to 35 miles per hour. The loss of life and the personal injuries are very much regretted. The cause of the accident is being investigated. The trestle was promptly repaired and the first train passed over it at 9:10 a.m. this morning."

The following is what I have been able to find about the "Wreck of Old 97" as well as her crew and the area in and around where the wreck took place.

The Crew

Killed:

Engineer Joseph A. Broady	Dead at the Scene
Fireman A.D. Clapp	Dead at the Scene
Apprentice Fireman Hodge	Dead at the Scene
Conductor J. Thomas Blair	Dead at the Scene
Flagman J.R. Moody	Dead at the Scene
Safe Locker Wentworth Armistead	Dead at the Scene
Postal Clerk J.L. Thompson	Dead at the Scene
Postal Clerk W.S. Chambers	Dead at the Scene
Postal Clerk D.P. Flory	Dead at the Scene
Postal Clerk P.M. Argenbright	Dead at the Scene
Postal Clerk L.W. Spies	Died of shock on October 6, 1903

Injured:

Postal Clerk J.J. Dunlap	Survived
Postal Clerk J. Harris Thompson	Survived
Postal Clerk N.C. Maupin	Survived
Postal Clerk Charles E. Reams	Survived
Postal Clerk Percival Indermauer	Survived
Postal Clerk Frank F. Brooks	Survived

Express Messenger W.F. Pinkney was the only one to escape without a scratch. He decided that one train wreck would last him for a whole lifetime and that he wasn't going to take any more chances, so he went directly to his home in Charlotte, N.C., and wrote out his resignation that same day.

Even before the disaster, Old 97 had an exciting history. One night, for instance, her wooden engine cab caught fire and was badly charred before the engine crew, seeking safety on the running board, managed to quench the blaze. Despite the emergency, they pulled into their terminal right on time. It was almost a religion with the crew that this high-speed train be kept on time.

Like many other wrecks that occurred on a Sunday, the wreck of the 97 was due in a large part to fast running. That day, various delays along the line caused the Southern's favorite train to reach Monroe, Va., 165 miles south of Washington, an hour late. Monroe is a division point, and crews are changed there. Joseph A. Broady mounted the deck of 1102 for her run south. Joe had the nickname "Steve," after the much-publicized Steve Brodie, who had won a bet by reputedly jumping off the Brooklyn Bridge several years before.

Old 97 was an hour late when the fresh crew took charge at Monroe. Joe, according to the song, was instructed to "get her into Spencer on time." But this verse is wrong, since the dispatcher did not order him to put her into Spencer on time. From Monroe to Spencer is 166 miles, and the fast mail's normal running time between the two points was about four hours and 15 minutes. Joe was expected to shave this down as much as possible, but even if the wreck had not occurred, it is improbable that he could have cut the time by as much as one hour and put the "hotshot" back on schedule.

One of the saddest features of the wreck was the fact that Wentworth Armistead was on the train by accident. He was only 17 and was employed by the Southern Express Company of Lynchburg. His duty was to lock the safe on the train after the valuables had been deposited in it and then get off. But on that Sunday, the train started suddenly and attained a high rate of speed before he could get off — so he rode straight through to his death. His body was not recovered until Tuesday morning, because he was buried underneath the pile of splintered cars.

On Friday, October 2, the body of Wentworth Armistead was taken back to Lynchburg for burial. The remains were accompanied by the young man's brother and mother. The bereaved mother obtained a window seat on the side of the car that would give her a view of the wreck as the train passed over the bridge. Knowing that this could only add to his mother's sorrow, the brother reached over and pulled down the shade as the train neared the scene of the disaster.

The main line of the Southern was moved several miles to the east in 1915, and the new roadbed very seldom touches the old. Stillhouse Trestle was torn down in 1934, but the trestle cut is still there. To the east of the cut, in the woods, some of the track can still be found, as well as an old handcar.

The station at Lynchburg is still in use today, as is the station in Danville. In 1915 the Danville station was moved in one piece by the use of mules and dollies to the site were it now stands. It was turned over to Amtrak in 1982.

The station at Fall Creek is also still standing, but today it is a steak house. This station was built circa 1890 and was closed in 1916 after the tracks were moved. The roadbed of the old line is still in front of the building.

The engine was a heavy 4-6-0 ten-wheeler, built by the Baldwin Locomotive Works (No. 22633) in 1903, and was in service only six months when the wreck occurred. She was removed from the wreck site by means of a temporary spur track that was laid from a point just south of the trestle, down into the ravine. After the wreck, the engine was returned to Baldwin for repairs and was later renumbered 1134. She continued to give faithful service until she fell under the cutter's torch at Princeton, Ind., in July 1935.

"Wreck of the Old 97"

On a cold frosty morning in the month of September
When the clouds were hanging low.
Ninety-seven pulled out of Washington Station
Like an arrow shot from a bow.

Oh, they handed him his orders at Monroe, Virginia,
Saying Steve, you're a-way behind time.
This is not thirty-eight, but it's old ninety-seven.
You must get her into Spencer on time.

It's a mighty rough road from Lynchburg to Danville,
And at Lima, there's a three-mile grade.
It was on this grade that he lost his airbrakes,
And you can see what a jump he made.

He was going downhill at ninety miles an hour,
When his whistle broke into a scream,
He was found in the wreck with his hand on the throttle,
And a-scalded to death by the steam.

Word arrived at Washington Station
And this is how it read,
The brave engineer that pulled Old 97
Is lying in Danville dead.

(Anonymous)

With most of the wreckage gone, the engine is made ready for removal. This photo was taken on Thursday, October 1, 1903.

– Norfolk Southern Corp.

Eng 1236 Mohawk Sept 1909

Southern Railway No. 41 westbound between Midway and Mohawk, Tenn., Engine 1236 Ps2, September 1909. Engineer was killed.
– Collection of Fred W. Bruce.

The New Market, Tenn., wreck, engine 1061, 4-6-0, and 1838, 4-4-0. Photo shows drivers of 1838 and wreckage, September 24, 1904.
– Collection of Fred W. Bruce.

Tragedy was to strike again at the Southern on November 29, 1906, when the railway's president, Samuel Spencer, was killed in a rear-end crash.

In the early morning hours of Thanksgiving Day, this railway horror was enacted on the Southern about 57 miles north of Danville, Va. Seven men met their doom. Killed in the horror was enacted on the Southern about 57 miles north of Danville, Va. Seven men met their doom. Killed in theRedwood of Baltimore; Charles D. Fisher of Baltimore; W.D. Davis of Alexandria, Va.; J.W. Shaw of Spencer, N.C.; and an unknown man.

President Spencer and his wealthy guests were on their way to the Carolinas for a hunting trip. The scene of the wreck was about a mile north of Lawyers, a small station on the Southern main line, and about nine miles south of Lynchburg. It was due, from all indications, to the carelessness of the operator at a block station, who allowed Number 37, the solid Pullman train, to pass into the block and crash into Number 33, President Spencer's train. Number 33 was a mixed Pullman and coach train. The time of the accident was between 6:10 and 6:20 a.m., while it was still dark and nearly all of the occupants of the two trains were still asleep, except the crews.

Number 33, consisting of a mail and express car, baggage car, a colored-passenger coach, a white-passenger coach, two Pullman cars, and a private car owned and used by President Spencer, was running behind time. The train was delayed at Lynchburg for an hour on account of some trouble with a drawbar to one of the coaches. The damage was repaired, and it was thought it would be sufficient for the train to reach as far as Greensboro, N.C. After the train had reached a point on the top of a high embankment a mile beyond Lawyers, more trouble was experienced with the drawbar and a stop was made.

Number 37, a solid Pullman train consisting of seven cars, was also running behind time, from New

Southern No. 1305, 4-6-2 turned over at Spring Street, Macon Ga., 1912.

— Collection of Fred W. Bruce.

York to New Orleans, and was following close behind Number 33. Operator Mattux at Rangoon, a block station about three miles north of where the accident occurred, had obtained a clear block for Number 33, and the train passed his station, as the records show, at four minutes past six. He then gave a clear block to the operator at Wilmer, the next block station, about three miles north, for a clear track for Number 37, which passed at five minutes past six. The block at Rangoon then showed that Operator Mattux did not receive a clear block from Lawyers, the next block south. Neither did it show that Number 33 had been reported as passing Lawyers. The Rangoon operator had not received a clear block for Number 37 to enter the block behind Number 33, following it by ten minutes.

There is a sharp grade downhill from Rangoon to Lawyers, with several curves. While Number 33 was standing on the track awaiting repairs, the flagman was sent back to signal the next train coming south to stop. The flagman said that before he could walk back far enough to give a proper signal, Number 37 came rushing around the bend and it was too late for him to avert a wreck.

While speeding over the rails at 30 miles an hour, Number 37 crashed into the rear of Number 33, which was at a complete standstill on the track. The engine of Number 37 plowed through the luxurious and elegantly furnished private car of President Spencer, where he and his guests were asleep. An explosion was heard for miles around due to the large gas tanks that were located under the private car (gas was used for lighting), and this was followed by a burst of flames. The fire spread quickly through the cars.

The conductor and a black porter began to rescue the passengers from the burning wreckage. Mr. F.M. Curtis of Jamestown, Ohio, was an inspiration for many others, helping rescue fellow passengers.

President Spencer, Schuyler, Fisher and Redwood were killed instantly, and all but Mr. Schuyler were charred practically beyond recognition.

Georgia Southern & Florida wreck of *Swanee River* Special below Valdosta, Ga., in 1912. Engine 501, 4-6-2. Engineer was killed. — *Collection of Fred W. Bruce.*

A cry for help came from beneath the burning wreckage of President Spencer's car. It was Mr. W.D. Davis, the president's private dispatcher. He was pinned beneath the iron girders, and when pulled out he was dying. His death, which he knew was close at hand, judging from the words he uttered, was pathetic and it brought tears to the cheeks of those in whose embrace he was held. He suffered the most excruciating pain, and his last words were a prayer for his wife and family.

The citizens residing near the scene of the wreck hastened with axes and other implements that would be of service. Wrecking crews arrived on the scene from Franklin Junction and Lynchburg, the Norfolk & Western sent a derrick crew from Norfolk, and a Southern derrick crew came from Monroe.

The wreck was not without remarkable incidents and thrilling escapes from death. How Mr. Will A. Kinney of Spencer, N.C., the engineer on Number 37, and his fireman (name unknown) escaped death is not known. Kinney stuck to his post and escaped with a few minor injuries.

Engine No. 1670 wrecked in West Yards, Knoxville, Tenn., January 2, 1910. Engineer William Hagues was killed.

— Collection of Fred W. Bruce.

Georgia Southern & Florida RR No. 117, 4-4-0 and 5 cars near Valdosta, Ga., July 1903.

– Collection of Fred W. Bruce.

Southern No. 362, 2-8-0 built by Baldwin in 1901.

– Collection of Fred W. Bruce.

Georgia Southern & Florida Ry. "Picnic Train" 1907 at Big Indian, Ga. Engines 154 and 152 both 4-4-0's.

Marietta & North
Georgia R.R. No. 4,
4-6-0 narrow gauge,
Baldwin built in 1887.
— *Collection of*
Fred W. Bruce.

This photo of Southern engine No. 1111 was taken on November 11, 1911 on the railway's Harrisonburg Branch.
— *Norfolk Southern Corp.*

For a number of years, this Southern switcher worked the railway's Monroe, Va., yard. Photo was taken in 1912.
- Norfolk Southern Corp.

Southern No. 3770, 4-4-0 at South Richmond, Va., February 1912.
- Collection of Fred W. Bruce.

Kestler Bridge, Over 90 Feet High and 500 Feet Long, Statesville, N. C.

Kestler Bridge, over 90 feet high and 500 feet long, Statesville, N.C. on Southern's Winston-Salem Div., 1914.

- G. Howard Gregory.

Southern Ry. 4-4-0.

- Collection of Fred W. Bruce.

Bostain Bridge,
Statesville, N. C.

Southern Railway's Asheville Div. A light Pacific crosses the Bostain Bridge on February 26, 1914.

- G. Howard Gregory.

Southern No. 635, 4-6-0.

- Collection of Fred W. Bruce.

Southern No. 315, 2-8-0 at Knoxville, Tenn., 1915.

– Collection of Fred W. Bruce.

Southern No. 3412, 2-6-0, a Mogul type at Richmond, Va., February 1916.

– Collection of Fred W. Bruce.

66

Southern No. 1914, 4-4-2 Atlantic type at Inman Yard, Atlanta. She was the last of the 4-4-2's to be cut up at Inman, July 19, 1940.
– Collection of Fred W. Bruce.

Southern (CNO&TP) No. 6422, 4-6-0 at Ludlow, Ky., 1919. Engineer C.H. Henderson on CNO&TP was running engine 6312 when it hit head-on with engine 6422 on a bridge in 1923. 6422 and 6312 were rebuilt and put back into service.
– Collection of Fred W. Bruce.

Passenger train No. 132 of the Atlantic & Yadkin Railway at Mt. Airy, N.C., Yard in 1922.

- Norfolk Southern Corp.

Southern No. 1911, 4-4-2 at Brunswick, Ga., September 1923.   – *Collection of Fred W. Bruce.*

Southern No. 22, 2-8-0 at Knoxville, Tenn., August 1923.   – *Collection of Fred W. Bruce.*

On January 1, 1918, pursuant to a proclamation by the President of the United States, all railways passed under the control of the United States Railroad Administration and were operated accordingly until March 1, 1920. During this period, as with all railroads in the country, Southern's property was not kept up to its usual standard, and upon being returned to the owners required heavy expenditures for deferred maintenance.

On January 31, 1922, Southern lost their passenger station in Danville, Va., to fire. The station was about 30 years old when fire broke out between 5:00 and 5:30 on Sunday morning. The fire apparently secured a hold in the space between the first-floor roof and the high gable, then it spread rapidly both ways and lit up the whole town. The loss was estimated at about $40,000. By noon Sunday a temporary ticket office was built of rough lumber in the subway, and while no tickets could be sold, as the supply had been destroyed by the fire, passengers were permitted to buy their tickets on the train without having to pay excess.

The Danville fire department had a hard time getting to the fire due to the fact that it had been snowing in Danville for a solid 36 hours, but they made all the speed that they could. The fire appeared to have its inception over the dining room, which was destroyed. The ticket office was burned, also the white and colored waiting rooms, the baggage room and the entire superstructure, including the tower in the middle. The firemen concentrated their efforts on saving the extreme northeastern wing of the building, and by hard work, they actually prevented the express office from being damaged. Little could be saved from the building, which appeared to have been burning for a long time before the fire alarm sounded.

In 1925, the pride of the Southern Railway was inaugurated: the *Crescent Limited*. Today's Amtrak *Crescent* is the lineal descendant of the *Washington and Southwestern Vestibuled Limited*, inaugurated in January 1891 by the Richmond & Danville Railroad, along the Piedmont Air Line Route. This Washington-to-Atlanta train was soon nicknamed the *Vestibule* because it was the first all-year train with vestibuled equipment in the South.

Soon the Washington-Atlanta schedule expanded to include a through Pullman to New Orleans via Montgomery and Mobile, Ala., over the rails of the Western Railway of Alabama and the Louisville & Nashville Railroad. New York was brought into the schedule via a connection with the Pennsylvania Railroad's *Congressional Limited*. Scheduled time for the New York-New Orleans run was advertised as a "40 hour, unprecedented trip." Because of the popularity of this through service, the *Washington and Southwestern Vestibuled Limited* became a solid train of through cars between New York and New Orleans. It carried the first dining cars to operate between those two cities.

Operation of the *Vestibule* continued after the Southern Railway was incorporated in 1894 by the purchasers of the Richmond & Danville. When vestibules became commonplace on long-distance trains, the title was shortened to *Washington and Southwestern Limited*. After 1900, through sleeping-cars (for Tampa, Fla., and Nashville, Tenn.) were added, and for the first time in its history, the *Limited* carried coaches (between New York and Atlanta.)

After operating 15 years as a solid train, in 1906 it was renamed the *New York and New Orleans Limited* and re-equipped with new observation and club cars. It became "a year-round exclusive Pullman car train." Coast-to-coast passengers, in connection with the Southern Pacific's *Sunset Express* via New Orleans, were actively solicited.

A new service was begun in 1925, and the train was renamed the *Crescent Limited*. On April 26, with the clock of the St. Louis Cathedral in New Orleans striking 10 p.m., a graceful Louisville & Nashville Pacific Class K-2 of pre-World War I vintage pulled out of Canal Street Station on her maiden trip. This deluxe, extra-fare all-Pullman consist ran solidly between New Orleans and New York over the Louisville & Nashville, the West Point Route, the Southern and the Pennsylvania railroads.

The *Crescent Limited* had luxurious Pullman equipment of the latest design, arranged to provide optimum comfort and convenience. The club car was forward, with movable easy chairs. Passengers lounged, smoked and chatted, with a valet-porter always nearby to assure comfort.

After July of 1926, the *Crescent Limited* was pulled between Atlanta and Washington by Southern's new green-and-gold heavy Pacific locomotives, Ps4 Class, each decorated with a gold crescent and the train's name emblazoned on the tender. Locomotive fanciers agree that those handsome iron horses rank among the most beautiful of them all.

Electrically illuminated tail signs were installed on the train's new observation sleepers. Rectangular in shape, the signs had a dark blue background showing a field of stars and the name *Crescent Limited* in white.

This is the famous *Crescent Limited* on the Southern Railway's main line. When she was inaugurated, she was an all-Pullman train. The engine was a Ps4 Pacific type painted in green and gold. This photo was taken near Greenville, S.C., in 1926.

– Collection of Fred W. Bruce.

This is one of the big Pacific Ps4's that pulled the *Crescent Limited* on Southern Railway's main line between Washington, D.C., and New Orleans, La. This photo was taken in 1926, in South Carolina.

– Norfolk Southern Corp.

The idea of painting Southern locomotives a beautiful green with gleaming gold accent stripes did not come from an advertising man. It came from Fairfax Harrison, president of Southern at the time. During a visit to England, he was favorably impressed by the popularity and beauty of green as a locomotive color. He particularly admired the medium shade of green used on the Southern Railway (of England) and the lighter apple-green of the London & North Eastern.

Southern Railway announced in 1929 that its first "train of luxury" was to begin life anew with brand-new equipment. Along with new Pullmans, cars built especially for the *Crescent Limited* four years earlier were completely refinished. What was "all new" was the distinctive exterior finish. Two shades of green adorned the luxury cars, each one lettered *Crescent Limited* in gold leaf along the upper panels. Pullman cars were named for the distinguished sons of the seven states of the South through which the train ran.

During the Great Depression, the name *Crescent Limited*, along with the extra fare and apple-green-colored train, vanished from the timetable. Southern Railway thought it best to "soft-pedal" its luxurious headliner during those severe times. In 1934, the name *Crescent Limited* was officially discontinued. Mr. Dillon Graham of New Orleans had this to say about the last run of the *Crescent Limited* in 1934: "Within every railroader there is sentiment and romance attached to trains. With the *Crescent's* proud history, it would have been less majestic to ask her to take to the roadbed as just another train, and not the accepted Queen of the Line. So the fast limited, with its famed identifying green-colored cars, was honorably withdrawn from service."

After the name *Crescent Limited* was discontinued, the trains were given run numbers 37 and 38 (for the north and south runs), and coaches were added to the consist. But in 1938, the train was renamed the *Crescent* and air-conditioned coach equipment, the first on the Southern, was added.

The late 1930s and 1940s saw the rise of the diesel on the Southern Railway. Following its first purchase of six two-car diesel-electric passenger units in 1939, the railway added its first diesel switching locomotives in 1940. In 1941, the Southern introduced to travelers two fine diesel-powered streamliners, *The Southerner* and *The Tennessean*, and the same year purchased the world's first four-unit diesel road freight locomotive after the 5,400 h.p. unit had completed a demonstration tour of the country's railroads.

The next step in the *Crescent's* history came in 1941 with the substitution of diesel power for steam between Atlanta and Washington. Strikingly attired in green, silver and gold, the new 4,000 h.p. General Motors units hauled the train south of Washington, while the Pennsylvania Railroad's electric locomotives handled the train between Washington and New York.

With dieselization, the *Crescent* was delivered by Pullman Standard. This new streamliner provided the latest in modern, comfortable, safe, all-weather transportation. A worthy successor to its famed predecessors, the train offered accommodations to meet every travel need.

Unfortunately, however, with passenger traffic continually being eroded by automobiles and airplanes, the years after 1950 saw the consolidation of many of the passenger routes. In 1967, the *Crescent*, which had operated as train Nos. 37 and 38, began to operate as Nos. 1 and 2 when it was consolidated with the *Southerner*. It was then renamed the *Southern Crescent* and offered dining car service between Washington and New Orleans, also reserved reclining-seat coaches and sleeping cars between New York and New Orleans.

From 1958, the engines of the Southern's premiere train were black and white, but President W. Graham Claytor, Jr. had the engines repainted in the green and gold of their proud ancestors in 1972. These engines wore the green and gold until they passed to Amtrak in 1979. (This would be the last chapter in the story of a fine passenger service that began with the old "Piedmont Air Line Route.")

A carefully worked out plan for preserving railroad passenger service between Washington, D.C., Atlanta, Ga., and New Orleans, La., that had been agreed to by Southern and the management of Amtrak failed to receive the approval of Amtrak's board of directors on March 1, 1978.

When Amtrak began operations in 1971, Southern chose to continue its passenger service, but by the late 1970s Southern filed to discontinue the *Piedmont*, one of their two remaining passenger trains. On November 28, 1976, the *Piedmont* made its last run from Washington to Charlotte, N.C.

On March 6, 1978, Southern filed to the ICC to discontinue its last passenger train, the *Southern Crescent*, because it was accruing losses at the rate of $560,000 a month. Southern could have filed for discontinuance of all service in 1974, but President L. Stanley Crane said that by operating the *Southern Crescent* and other quality trains for several years, Southern had gone the extra mile in fulfilling its common carrier obligations. Mr. Crane said: "The thought of having to give up this fine train is as personally distressing to me as it is to its loyal fans. However, I take some consolation in the knowledge that it did not fail for lack of interest or effort on our part. I am proud of the effort we made and only regret that our best was not good enough."

On May 2, 1978, the ICC started public hearings in Washington, D.C., which ended on June 14 in New Orleans, La. The ICC made its decision on Southern's application on August 4, 1978: that the Southern Railway continue to operate the *Crescent* for a period of one year, after which time, if Southern still wished to discontinue service, it would again have to seek commission approval.

By mid-December of 1978, Amtrak and Southern reached an agreement for Amtrak to take over operation of the *Southern Crescent*. Effective February 1, 1979, the control passed to Amtrak and it became the *Amtrak Crescent*.

A Mikado steam engine once used on the Southern, No. 4866 was built in 1928. Photo was taken near Atlanta in 1933.
— *Norfolk Southern Corp.*

Southern No. 1455, 4-8-2 at Morristown, Tenn. She was named "King of them All" because of the best coal and performance record on the Knoxville Div. 1933.

– Collection of Fred W. Bruce.

Southern No. 3002, 2-6-0 (Mogul type) at Atlanta, Ga., September 1934. She was scrapped at Hayne, S.C., November 1939.

– Collection of Fred W. Bruce.

Engine No. 4880, a 2-8-2 type waits for orders in Charlotte, N.C., 1938.
— *Photo by Frank E. Ardrey, Jr.*

Southern (CNO&TP) No. 6491, 4-8-2 at Chattanooga, Tenn., June 1937.   — *Collection of Fred W. Bruce.*

A merchandise freight train of the Southern Railway leaving Meridian, Miss.   - *Norfolk Southern Corp.*

Southern (AGS) Ps4 No. 6688 at Birmingham, Ala., 1939.
- *Collection of Frank E. Ardrey, Jr.*

76

A Southern Ps4 No. 1395 poses for its photo, March 25, 1938.

- G. Howard Gregory.

On May 3, 1933, Southern Railway's freight train Number 52 left the rails at Stacey Curve, half a mile south of Ruffin, N.C. (11 miles south of Danville, Va.), injuring eight people and scores of cattle. Railway and city police investigated a report that a spike had been placed on the rail by a child.

Mr. L.O. Woodson, fireman on Number 52, said, "The train was running about 50 miles an hour when it left the rails. The first I knew of any trouble was when I felt the truck wheels bumping on the cross-ties and, looking ahead, saw rails flying upward, ripped from the track. The entire scene was so obscured with hissing steam that I could not find my way from the wreckage for some time." Finally he saw an opening in the steam and headed for it, only to be struck by some object and knocked almost senseless. Upon recovering, Mr. Woodson failed to see the engineer and started back into the steam to find him, but was met by a railroad detective and a trainman bringing out the unconscious engineer. The engineer was scalded over an extensive area of his body, and he had inhaled escaping steam, which had injured his throat. Physicians said that there was danger of pneumonia in his weakened condition.

The train was en route to New York with a load of cattle and chickens, but after the derailment a number of the fine beef cattle had to be shot to prevent them from suffering.

The tracks were cleared for use of traffic, as work crews from Danville, Spencer and Monroe labored with the aid of three wrecking derricks to remove the wreckage.

Mr. George Allen, engineer of Number 52, was buried on Sunday, May 7, 1933, with a large number of fellow railroad men from all departments attending. Mr. L.O. Woodson recovered from his injuries.

The child who derailed the train admitted to detectives that he had done it. No charges were filed against the child for his actions. While still in the hospital, Mr. Woodson said he would like to talk to the boy and characterized as ridiculous the idea that he might bear ill will against him. He said he realized, of course, that the boy could not have had any intention of wrecking the train.

Mobile & Ohio No. 55, a 0-6-0 type.

– Collection of Frank E. Ardrey, Jr.

Tallulah Falls No. 75 at Cornelia, Ga., a 2-6-0 type.

– Photo by R.E. Prince, Jr., collection of Frank E. Ardrey, Jr.

No. 6100, the world's first diesel-electric road freight locomotive hauling a Southern freight train south over the old Cumberland River Bridge near Burnside, Ky. This bridge has since been replaced with a newer and higher one. The site of the one shown here is now under the waters of the Wolf Creek Dam Reservoir.

- Norfolk Southern Corp.

In April 1945, the Southern, the Pennsylvania, and the New York Central had the sad duty of taking the body of President Franklin D. Roosevelt home to Hyde Park, New York.

President Roosevelt's last trip to Warm Springs, Ga., was on the 28th of March 1945. His special train then returned to Atlanta, where it was cleaned, inspected and restocked. It was always ready to move on short notice.

On April 12, the news was flashed over the radio that President Roosevelt was dead. That was 3:35 p.m. and by 6:00 p.m. the men at the roundhouse were busy getting two Pacifics ready to go. At 9:45 p.m. Superintendent W.F. Cooper, Trainmaster A.W. St. Clair and Conductor Emmit Whittle came solemnly down the Track 10 stairway. The skipper had the last running orders for the President's train in his hand.

The train left Warm Springs at 11:13 a.m. on the 13th for Washington, D.C. On the run between Warm Springs and Atlanta, the engine crews were ordered to "run slow, run silent." There were ten Pacific locomotives used to pull this special from Georgia to Washington, D.C., they were: from Warm Springs to Atlanta, Nos. 1262 and 1337; from Atlanta to Greenville, S.C., Nos. 1409 and 1394; from Greenville, S.C. to Salisbury, N.C., Nos. 1401 and 1385; from Salisbury, N.C. to Monroe, Va., Nos. 1400 and 1367; from Monroe, Va., to Washington, D.C., Nos. 1406 and 1366. The train pulled into Union Station exactly at 10:00 a.m. on April 14, 1945.

In a modernization effort, the Southern began a wholesale replacement of steam locomotives with diesel-electric engines in 1946. By the end of World War II, Southern had 155 diesel units in service; they had done yeoman work for America's victory. But that was only the beginning. In 1948, Southern almost doubled the number of diesel locomotives of all types, and all but tripled the size of its freight diesel fleet. By the end of 1949, the Southern had 520 diesels, and with the outbreak of the Korean War in 1950, Southern was ready again with the motive power for its share of the increased transportation job required.

Complete dieselization of the Southern — the last regular run of a steam locomotive anywhere on the railway — came on June 17, 1953, when Engine 6330 chugged to a stop at Chattanooga and had the fire knocked from the firebox for the last time.

The building and improvement program that has made the Southern practically a new railroad since 1946 extends into every branch of railway operation. Many millions of dollars have been spent on ultra-modern freight classification yards such as Sevier Yard at Knoxville, Tenn., Norris Yard in Birmingham, Ala., and also new yards at Chattanooga, Tenn., Atlanta, Ga., and Linwood, N.C. New diesel shops have been built and older shops remodeled to take care of system-wide diesel running repair and maintenance. Wide use is being made of electronic aids to railway operations, such as end-to-end radio on through freight trains, radio and loudspeaker communications in freight yards, and centralized traffic control (CTC).

Southern Nos. 1853 & 1850, 0-8-0 type at the south end of Inman Yard, Atlanta, 1940.

– Photo by R.D. Sharpless, collection of Frank E. Ardrey, Jr.

Norfolk Southern No. 600, a 2-8-4 type at Norfolk, Va., 1940.   – *Photo by R.E. Prince, Jr., collection of Frank. E. Ardrey, Jr.*

Norfolk Southern No. 110, a 4-6-0 type at Norfolk, Va., 1940.   – *Photo by R.E. Prince, Jr., collection of Frank. E. Ardrey, Jr.*

Freight engine double-heading No. 3 *Royal Palm* up hill from Ludlow, Ky., to Erlanger, Ky. Freight engine then returns to Ludlow Yard, 1940.

– *G. Howard Gregory.*

Tennessee Central No. 50 at Nashville, Tenn., this is an early ALCO switcher, 1940.

– *Photo by R.D. Sharpless, collection of F.E. Ardrey, Jr.*

Southern No. 3, engine 6482, *Royal Palm* climbing Erlanger Hill, 2 miles south of Ludlow, Ky., 1940.

– G. Howard Gregory.

Mobile & Ohio No. 480, a 2-8-2 at Birmingham, Ala., 1940.   *– Collection of Frank E. Ardrey, Jr.*

Southern No. 1256, on the Murphy branch coming off bridge and curve at Governors Island, N.C., 1947.

– Photo by R.D. Sharpless, collection of Frank E. Ardrey, Jr.

Danville and Western No.
20 standing beside the shop
in Danville, Va., 1940.

– Author's collection.

Danville and Western No. 22. The people in Danville nicknamed the D&W the "Dick and Willie." Photo was
made in the 1940s in Danville, Va.

– Author's collection.

Southern engines 4761 and 4578, both 2-8-2's wrecked at Spartanburg, S.C., in a head-on crash.
– Collection of Fred W. Bruce.

Boiler explosion on engine 4873 in 1942, near Red Lane, Ga. Engineer and fireman were hurt. Extra 4873 south cut loose from its train and ran to Gainesville to take on water. Then returned to its train and started off, after 3 miles up-grade the crown sheet gave way.
– Collection of Fred W. Bruce.

Southern Ry. Boiler Explosion, engine No. 4828, 2-8-2 near Lula, Ga., December 1944. The engineer, fireman and brakeman were all killed. Photo shows engine being dragged away from burning tank and cars. The brakeman was found under debris, in the coal, 3 days after the explosion. Cause of the explosion was low water, crown sheet failure.

– Collection of Fred W. Bruce.

CNO&TP engine 816, a 4-6-2 wrecked at Anadel, Tenn.

– Collection of Fred W. Bruce.

Central of Georgia No. 456 leaving Birmingham Terminal Station pulling the *Seminole* southbound in 1946.

- Photo by Frank E. Ardrey, Jr.

Southern 6922 waits next to the round-house at Meridian, Miss., 1946.

- Photo by C.W. Witbeck, collection of Frank E. Ardrey, Jr.

Blue Ridge No. 3458 at Hayne Shop, Spartanburg, S.C., in 1946.
– *Photo by C.W. Witbeck, collection of Frank E. Ardrey, Jr.*

Southern No. 4053, 2-8-8-2, westbound at Chattahoochee, Ga., for Birmingham, 1946.
– *Photo by R.D. Sharpless, collection of Frank E. Ardrey, Jr.*

Southern No. 6636, 2-8-2 (Ex-Erie) bought by Southern in 1941, then rebuilt at Finley Shop, Birmingham, Ala.

– Collection of Fred W. Bruce.

Southern 1462, 4-8-2 Ts Class at Finley, Ala., September 2, 1946.

– Collection of Fred W. Bruce.

Southern No. 949, 4-6-0 at Selma, Ala., September 1, 1946. She was scrapped at Hayne, S.C., December 1950.
– Collection of Fred W. Bruce.

Southern No. 1257, 4-6-2 at Macon, Ga., April 28, 1946. She was an ex-Knoxville Div. engine and she was scrapped in 1949.
– Collection of Fred W. Bruce.

Southern No. 6318, 2-8-2 at Citico, Tenn., 1946.

- Collection of Fred W. Bruce.

Southern Nos. 1461 and 1483, 4-8-2 Ts and Ts1 Class engines pulling the *Kansas City-Florida Special* No. 7
with iron furnaces in background at Birmingham, 1946.

- Photo by Frank E. Ardrey, Jr.

Southern No. 4153, F-3 units on a reverse curve westbound at Douglasville, Ga., 1947.
- Photo by R.D. Sharpless, collection of Frank E. Ardrey, Jr.

Southern No. 40, the *Vulcan* one of only six Fairbanks Morse diesel-powered units of this type, Birmingham, 1946.
- Photo by Frank E. Ardrey, Jr.

Tallulah Falls No. 78 crossing a long trestle at Tallulah Falls, Ga. Note the old-style boxcars.
- Photo by R.D. Sharpless, collection of Frank E. Ardrey, Jr.

Southern (AGS) No. 6695, 4-8-2 at Birmingham, 1946.
- Photo by Frank E. Ardrey, Jr.

Southern No. 4054, 2-8-8-2 Ls2 Class, at Inman Yard, Atlanta, 1946.   – *Photo by R.D. Sharpless, collection of Frank E. Ardrey, Jr.*

Southern No. 6693, No. 39 Sunnyland near Austell, Ga., 1947.   – *Photo by R.D. Sharpless, collection of Frank E. Ardrey, Jr.*

Southern No. 1396 Ps4 at Washington, D.C., 1947.

- Photo by George E. Votava collection of Frank E. Ardrey, Jr.

Here an Interstate No. 23, 2-6-6-2 sits next to turntable pit in Andover, Va., 1947.

- Photo by R.E. Prince, Jr., collection of Frank E. Ardrey, Jr.

Southern No. 1256, 4-6-2 on Murphy branch local passenger No. 17 at Governors Island, N.C., 1947.

– Photo by R.D. Sharpless, collection of Frank E. Ardrey, Jr.

Southern No. 1545, 0-6-0 at Westminster, S.C., 1947.   *– Photo by R.D. Sharpless, collection of Frank E. Ardrey, Jr.*

Two Southern freights about to pass each other. The near train has FTs and the far train has F-3s. Photo was taken at South Inman, Atlanta, 1947.
- Photo by R.D. Sharpless, collection of Frank E. Ardrey, Jr.

Southern No. 2402 TR-2 "cow and calf" passes by engine No. 4575 at Inman Yard, Atlanta, 1947.

- Photo by R.D. Sharpless, collection of Frank E. Ardrey, Jr.

ALCO S-1 at Birmingham, the regular "shed" engine, at Birmingham Terminal Station, 1947.

– Photo by R.D. Sharpless, collection of Frank E. Ardrey, Jr.

ALCO S-2 Southern No. 2215 at Atlanta, 1947.   *– Photo by R.D. Sharpless, collection of Frank E. Ardrey, Jr.*

Southern No. 1380, 4-6-2, the only streamlined locomotive that Southern owned, 1947.

— *G. Howard Gregory.*

Here No. 1380, a Ps4 Class, pulls train No. 135 at Chamblee, Ga., 1947.

— *Photo by R.D. Sharpless, collection of Frank E. Ardrey, Jr.*

109.

Southerner view of train with round-end observation car showing old telegraph office at Weems, Ala. The two train order signals are for the Southern and the Central of Georgia; top signal for Southern to Atlanta, and the lower signal for the Central of Georgia to Columbus, 1948.

— *Photo by Frank E. Ardrey, Jr.*

Southern No. 4108, FT diesel 4 units eastbound at Weems, Ala., passing under telltales and entering crossover to single track, 1948.

— *Photo by Frank E. Ardrey, Jr.*

Blue Ridge No. 3, 4-6-0 pulls a mixed train, 1947.

- Photo by R.D. Sharpless, collection of Frank E. Ardrey, Jr.

Central of Georgia No. 642, 2-8-2 MK Class passing over timber trestle west of Newnan, Ga., 1948.

- Photo by R.D. Sharpless, collection of Frank E. Ardrey, Jr.

Southern No. 4827 climbing Gate City Hill (Red Mountain) near Irondale, Ala., 1948.

- Photo by Frank E. Ardrey, Jr.

Georgia, Southern & Florida (Southern) No. 8839, 2-8-0 at Macon, Ga., 1948.

- Photo by James Bowie, collection of Frank E. Ardrey, Jr.

End of the line for Southern No. 109 as she sits in scrap line at Inman Yard, Atlanta, 1948. Note that headlight has already been removed.

— Photo by R.D. Sharpless, collection of Frank E. Ardrey, Jr.

Southern No. 5230, 2-10-2 at Chattanooga, 1948.

— Photo by Frank E. Ardrey, Jr.

106

Southern No. 1509, 0-4-4T, at Atlanta, 1948. This was the shop engine at Pegram Shop and has been preserved.

- Photo by Frank E. Ardrey, Jr.

Southern No. 6495, 4-8-2 at Chattanooga, 1948.   *- Photo by Frank E. Ardrey, Jr.*

Interstate No. 2, 2-8-0 at Andover, Va., 1948.

- Photo by R.H. Kennedy, collection of Frank E Ardrey, Jr.

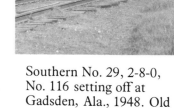

Southern No. 29, 2-8-0, No. 116 setting off at Gadsden, Ala., 1948. Old depot now torn down.

Central of Georgia No. 420, 4-6-2 at Augusta, Ga., 1948.

- Photo by R.E. Prince, Jr., collection of Frank E. Ardrey, Jr.

Southern Nos. 5045 and 5052, 2-10-2 leaving Melrose, N.C., at foot of Saluda Grade, 1948.

High Point, Randleman, Asheboro & Southern No. 317, 2-8-0. This was one of Southern's independent lines. Photo made at Greensboro, N.C., 1948.

Southern No. 1392, 4-6-2 Ps4 pulling train No. 135 at Lenox Road (Atlanta) 1949.

- Photo by R.D. Sharpless, collection of Frank E. Ardrey, Jr.

Rear of extra 4176 north on Nickajack Hill, near Atlanta, on long sweeping curve, 1948.

- Photo by R.D. Sharpless, collection of Frank E. Ardrey, Jr.

Southern F units pass by a line of locomotives at coal chute, Inman Yard, Atlanta, 1948.

– Photo by R.D. Sharpless, collection of Frank E. Ardrey, Jr.

Atlantic & Yadkin No. 444 at Pomona Yard, Greensboro, N.C., 1948.

– Photo by Frank E. Ardrey, Jr.

Central of Georgia No. 801, E-7 locomotive on streamliner *Man O'War* at East Point, Ga., 1949.

- Photo by Frank E. Ardrey, Jr.

Interstate No. 20, 2-8-8-2 at Norton, Va., 1949.   *- Photo by R.E. Prince, Jr., collection of Frank E. Ardrey, Jr.*

Southern extra 5023 west with helper 5045 and pusher 5047 at Saluda Hill in 1948. Saluda Hill is on a 4.7% grade. It is the steepest grade on any main line in the U.S.

– Photo by Frank E. Ardrey, Jr.

Southern No. 5047, 2-10-2 acts as a pusher on the rear of *Carolina Special* passenger train up Saluda Grade, 1950.

– Photo by R.D. Sharpless, collection of Frank E. Ardrey, Jr.

Southern No. 1387, 4-6-2 pulls No. 30 out of Atlanta with two F-3 diesels, 1950.

– Photo by R.D. Sharpless, collection of Frank E. Ardrey, Jr.

Southern No. 1406 is substituting for ailing diesel units on No. 47, the *Southerner* at Lenox Road, Atlanta, 1950.

- Photo by R.D. Sharpless, collection of Frank E. Ardrey, Jr.

Southern No. 4138, F-3 and F3b refueling at Atlanta Terminal Station, 1950.

- Photo by R.D. Sharpless, collection of Frank E. Ardrey, Jr.

Southern No. 1493, 4-8-2 Ts1 Class leaving Atlanta with train No. 30, the *Peach Queen* with helping diesels, 1951.

– Photo by R.D. Sharpless, collection of Frank E. Ardrey, Jr.

Two 4-6-2 Ps4 Class doubleheading train No. 20, express and mail train at Armour (Atlanta), 1951.

– Photo by R.D. Sharpless, collection of Frank E. Ardrey, Jr.

Southern Nos. 4899 and 4903, 2-8-2 doubleheading leaving Inman Yard, Atlanta, 1951.

- Photo by R.D. Sharpless, collection of Frank E. Ardrey, Jr.

Southern No. 5027 descending Saluda with a troop train, 1950.

– Photo by R.D. Sharpless, collection of Frank E. Ardrey, Jr.

"A streak of silver against a backdrop of autumn tinted trees," the *Crescent* rolling north across Wells Viaduct in the Georgia Hills just south of Toccoa, Ga., 1950. — *Norfolk Southern Corp.*

Central of Georgia Nos. 481, 4-8-2, and 776, 2-10-2, doubleheading between Smarr-Bolingbroke, Ga., pulling train No. 34, 1952. — *Photo by R.D. Sharpless, collection of Frank E. Ardrey, Jr.*

Southern No. 8337 has come to the last mile as she sits in scrap line, Atlanta, 1952.

- Photo by R.D. Sharpless, collection of Frank E. Ardrey, Jr.

Southern engines 1697, 1690, and 1704, all 0-6-0 switch engines in round-house at Inman Yard, Atlanta, 1951.

- Photo by R.D. Sharpless, collection of Frank E. Ardrey, Jr.

Southern Ry. Dead Engine Train — Diesel units 4259, 4422, 4423, and 4258 leave Inman Yard with engines 4764, 4752, 4754, 4759, 4714, 790, 1240, 6300, 6312, 6318, 6280, 6291, 6298 and 800 in tow, 1952.
    – Collection of Fred W. Bruce

Southern No. 1258 waits for the cutter's torch at Atlanta, 1952.   *– Photo by R. D. Sharpless, collection of Frank E. Ardrey, Jr.*

Southern No. 4176, F-7 three unit freight passing old coal chute at Lula, Ga., on train No. 156, 1951.

– Photo by R.D. Sharpless, collection of Frank E. Ardrey, Jr.

Southern No. 6541, GP-7 northbound at Constitution, Ga., with a military train, 1951.

– Photo by R.D. Sharpless, collection of Frank E. Ardrey, Jr.

122

Southern F units at fuel rack, Inman Yard, Atlanta, 1951.   *- Photo by R.D. Sharpless, collection of Frank E. Ardrey, Jr.*

Southern No. 6142, FP-7 northbound at Austell, Ga., pulling the *New Royal Palm* through interlocker, 1953.
     - Photo by R.D. Sharpless, collection of Frank E. Ardrey, Jr.

Tennessee Central No. 803, FA-1 westbound near Rockwood, Tenn. Train is coming out of a tunnel, 1953.

- Photo by R.D. Sharpless, collection of Frank E. Ardrey, Jr.

Central of Georgia No. 907, an F3, No. 145, an RS-3, and No. 131, a GP-9, pull a train near Griffin, Ga., 1954.
- Photo by R.D. Sharpless, collection of Frank E. Ardrey, Jr.

Tennessee Central FA-1's crossing bridge in mountains near Rockwood, Tenn. 1953.
- Photo by R.D. Sharpless, collection of Frank E. Ardrey, Jr.

Central of Georgia No. 103, FM H-15-44 local freight near Fort Valley, Ga., 1953.

– Photo by R.D. Sharpless, collection of Frank E. Ardrey, Jr.

Southern No. 4225, F-7 with a pair of GP units between the F's, westbound between Douglasville and Villa Rica, Ga., 1954.

– Photo by R.D. Sharpless, collection of Frank E. Ardrey, Jr.

AMERICAN LOCOMOTIVE COMPANY
NEW YORK CITY

Southern No. 2119, RS-2 built in 1949 by the American Locomotive Company in Schenectady, N.Y. The offices were in New York City.

- ALCO photo, collection of Walter Johnson.

Southern No. 2119, RS-2 passing Atlanta Terminal Station on transfer cut, 1953.

- Photo by R.D. Sharpless, collection of Frank E. Ardrey, Jr.

In 1957, North Carolina's century-old dream of an east-west railroad was finally realized when Southern took over operation of the Atlantic & East Carolina. They owe a lasting debt to John Motley Morehead's determination that "the road must be built."

Southern acquired control of the Central of Georgia on June 17, 1963, through purchase of the approximately 71 percent stock interest in the Central of Georgia which had been held by the St. Louis-San Francisco Railway.

Acquisition of the 1,912-mile Central of Georgia Railway and the 321-mile Georgia & Florida Railroad increased the mileage of the Southern Railway to 10,413.

Three Southern subsidiaries purchased the Georgia & Florida on June 29, 1963. The move ended a long period of uncertainty for the G&F, which had been in receivership for 44 of the previous 47 years.

Southern puts a lot of emphasis and effort on improved safety and accident prevention. They have won both the E.H. Harriman Memorial Award for employee safety and the Dow Chemical Award for superior performance in handling Dow products several times. They have also won numerous other awards for all kinds of safety programs.

It was a new kind of team that was put together in 1968 to minimize the hazards that may result when accidents do occur, especially if they involve various types of hazardous materials. This team is made up of specialists trained and equipped to help local officers deal with emergencies. They are called the "Go Team" because they are ready to go in minutes after an alarm is given. From their base in Atlanta, they can be on the road or in the air within an hour with a trailer-load of special equipment to help deal with emergency situations. Their special role is to help identify any hazardous materials involved in an accident and make sure that they can be dealt with safely.

The equipment they carry includes firefighting suits, acid suits and masks, respirators, test devices, first aid kits and special tools. The availability of such a team of specialists is part of an Emergency Action Plan that operates throughout the Southern system. And to make the plan work even more effectively, members of the Go Team train key officers on each operating division to deal safely with various kinds of potentially dangerous cargo. The plan for concentrating the skills of railway people to deal quickly with this sort of emergency has been so well received in the railroad industry that several other railroads are working on similar plans.

Southern also organized, in 1968, the "mobile agent." The first mobile agent route opened on the Central of Georgia in early September 1968. He worked out of a base station in Millen, Ga., and served seven nearby communities. Before the end of 1968, there was a second mobile agent at work, based in Chattanooga. The mobile agent carries the railroad's personalized service to the customers. He travels his territory equipped with a two-way radio, so that he is in frequent radio contact with his base office. His customers can get in touch with him at any time, and he is often in contact with train crews in the area. Also, he personally visits with shippers in the communities along his route, helping them with the preparation of bills of lading, routing of freight shipments, car supply and other needs. He can check customers' plant sidings personally and expedite the placing of empty cars and the pulling of loaded cars for movement to their destination. Since 1968, the mobile agent system has been in effect throughout the total Southern Railway System.

Also in 1968, the Tennessee Central was brought into the Southern. It was called the "Nashville Route" and was 248 miles long, running between Hopkinsville, Ky., and Harriman, Tenn. It was a bridge line between the Southern and the Louisville & Nashville railways, but in 1968 the Tennessee Central was abandoned and the line was divided between the Illinois Central, Southern, and the Louisville & Nashville.

In 1972, the executives of Southern Railway and Norfolk Southern Railway agreed to proceed with the merger of a Southern Railway subsidiary, the Carolina & Northwestern Railway, into the Norfolk Southern Railway (the old one). The merger application was put before the Interstate Commerce Commission, and in 1974 the Norfolk Southern was merged into the Southern Railway. (The name of the Norfolk Southern was changed on June 1, 1982, to the Carolina & Northwestern, so that its name would not be confused with that of its parent company.)

End of the "smoke and cinder" era on the 8,000 mile Southern came at Chattanooga, Tenn., on June 17, 1953. Engine No. 6330 rolled into the yard with smoke blasting and the whistle moaning a long farewell to the "Iron Horse".

- *Norfolk Southern Corp.*

Moving information is just as important as moving freight cars. As a matter of fact, information speeds the movement of freight cars, especially at Southern's computer-controlled classification yard near Sheffield, Ala., built in 1973.

The yard is four miles long and is on a 180-acre site five miles southeast of Sheffield. It contains about 45 miles of track. It can hold about 3,000 cars and eventually will classify up to 2,400 cars a day.

With the exception of run-through trains, all westbound traffic for Sheffield and beyond is classified at this yard, reducing the work load at Southern yards in Chattanooga and Birmingham. All of the eastbound traffic from Memphis and beyond is also classified, relieving pressure on Southern's yard in Memphis.

In 1974, the Interstate came into the Southern Railway, it was a short-line system 62 miles long that ran around the Norton, Va., area in the western part of the state.

In 1975, concerns for protection of the environment brought new air quality regulations in Georgia. Low-sulphur coals from Kentucky and the Midwest became very attractive. Southern and the Southern Companies decided to go ahead with a transloading venture, with Southern to build the transloader and the power company to lease or buy the facility. The transloader began operation in September 1977, and it includes a barge-mooring area at the riverbank, a high-speed bucket elevator that unloads the barges, belt conveyors and a traveling stacker to move coal into six massive storage piles.

Coal that is mined in Kentucky and Illinois moves by barge along the Mississippi, Ohio and Tennessee rivers to the transloader. Each barge is filled with 1,500 tons of coal and travels in tows of 2 to 15 units. At the transloader mooring, the bucket elevator unloads each barge in about 45 minutes. A movable stacker distributes coal to the six storage piles according to its sulphur content and other factors. When the coal is loaded onto a unit train for a particular power plant, the blend is a specific one that meets the plant's air quality and other requirements. This calls for specific amounts of coal from various piles. The coal then drops onto an underground conveyor belt, which moves it to the loader, and as a 97-car unit train moves slowly beneath the loader, each car in turn is loaded. The loading of this 97-car train takes about three and a half hours. When the unit train arrives at a power plant, it passes slowly over a trestle above the storage area. There each car dumps its coal through bottom doors, emptying the entire train in 30 minutes. There are several unit trains now in operation between the transloader and the power plants. These unit trains move on "cycles" between the mines, the transloader and the power plants that they serve. The unit trains are just one of Southern's many innovations.

In June 1979, Southern opened a new yard at Linwood, N.C., named Spencer Yard. It was the result of a careful computer study of freight movement patterns throughout the railway. Nine of the ten most congested flat yards were on the eastern lines, and five of them were fairly close to where the Spencer Yard is located. Since the yard opened, delays have been reduced and the transit time improved for smaller yards in Greensboro, Charlotte, and Asheville, N.C., and Spartanburg and Greenville, S.C., as well as the old yard at Spencer, N.C., which it replaced.

Other major yards with which Spencer Yard works in tandem (and the dates they were opened) are: Sevier Yard, Knoxville, Tenn. (1951); Norris Yard, Birmingham, Ala. (1952); DeButts Yard, Chattanooga, Tenn. (1955); Inman Yard, Atlanta, Ga. (1957); Brosnan Yard, Macon, Ga. (1967); and Sheffield Yard, Sheffield, Ala. (1973).

When Southern dedicated the new facility, they named it Spencer Yard in honor of Southern's first president, Samuel Spencer, thus perpetuating the memory and the pioneer spirit of the man for whom its historic (but now closed) Spencer Shops were named. The shops themselves, together with some 54 acres of land on which they are located, were presented by the Southern to the State of North Carolina, which is preserving and renovating the site as a transportation museum.

Spencer Yard is four and a half miles long, south of Linwood, in southern Davidson County, N.C. Southern's Atlanta-Washington main line skirts the yard to the east. The yard can receive, classify and reassemble into trains up to 3,000 cars a day. At the present time, there are 46 tracks in this yard, but if needed, there is room to expand the classification yard to 50 tracks.

Few people still travel by train. For every Amtrak passenger car that might be rolling on Southern's lines this minute, there are hundreds of freight cars in operation. But there are still plenty of people around who think that nothing quite compares with an old-fashioned train ride — for entertainment, that is, not for transportation. So, Southern often runs excursion trips with special trains drawn by vintage steam locomotives. A delightful experience in itself, the steam trip also serves as a reminder of just how far railroads have come since the days of the old steam locomotives that boasted such names as *Comet* or *Antelope*, or the grandaddy of them all, the *Best Friend of Charleston*, the wood-burning locomotive that started the first regularly scheduled steam-powered railroad service in America. And it operated on a line that is now part of Southern.

Today's diesel-electric locomotives wear numbers instead of names. They may not have the personality of the old steamers, but they started a quiet revolution that changed railroading. Southern bought the first diesel built for road freight service in this country and was the first major rail line to be 100 percent dieselized.

Today, Southern runs its railroad as a 9,966-mile-long assembly line producing modern transportation. This means using automated shop production techniques; highly mechanized track-laying and track maintenance; electronically controlled classifications yards; the largest private microwave communications network east of the Mississippi, with more than one and a quarter million miles of voice and data transmission circuits; computers that not only sort facts and figures at lightning speed but can simulate train and yard operations to help study proposed changes in facilities and techniques; intermodal transportation service blending the advantages of rail and highway or rail and water carriage; freight agents that take the railroad to the customer with radio-equipped vehicles; a continuing effort to help customers locate or relocate their plants along the railroad's lines; and a never-ending study of the transportation needs of their customers.

They call themselves "Southern Railing System," and they believe what they say in their slogan, the "Southern Serves the South." Their lines extend as far north as Washington, D.C., and Cincinnati, Ohio; as far west as East St. Louis, Ill., Memphis, Tenn., and New Orleans, La.; and as far south as Florida. In all, they have 9,966 miles of line in 13 states.

In an industry that has known more than its share of economic difficulties, Southern is successful, and has been for many years. Southern strives to be not just a railroad, but a "transportation company." Southern believes that any company earns its right to exist by constantly studying the needs of its customers and finding new ways to meet those needs.

Life in the South has been changing dramatically over the past 20 years, with the appearance of new industries, the growth of metropolitan areas and the vast expansion of the region as a market for goods and services of all kinds. Southern Railway has not only been keeping pace with this growth but, in many cases, has set the pace, helping initiate many of the changes that have strengthened the economy of the region they serve. Southern's industrial development people have been promoting the South's economic growth for many years.

Obviously, there's a payoff for Southern when a new plant locates along its lines. A new freight customer. But what does it mean for the community? Plenty! Jobs, of course, but that's only the start of it. New factories also mean more support and service industries, more money in local cash registers, rising bank deposits and a boost to the local economy.

Making friends and building a region, that's the Southern way.

On any given day, you can find many of Southern's salesmen and market researchers a long way from anything that looks like railroading. A major part of their work is to get to know their customers' businesses inside and out, so that Southern can come up with the new transportation services to suit their needs.

As a result of their studies, Southern has been able to provide faster, more reliable, more economical service to a variety of customers. Southern has designed new freight cars and taught old cars new tricks:

– For the lumber industry, a bulkhead flatcar designed for mechanized loading and unloading. It cuts the time for either of these operations to a couple of hours, compared with the two days it used to take to load or unload a conventional boxcar by hand.
– For grain shippers and users, the "Big John", a one-hundred-ton capacity aluminum-covered hopper car that helps to cut the cost of shipping bulk grain by 60 percent.
– For anybody in an industry with fragile freight to ship, the Super Cushion Car. Its hydraulically cushioned underframe, adapted by Southern engineers, absorbs jolts and jars to give the freight inside a smooth ride.
– For auto manufacturers, special auto parts trains from factories in the Midwest to assembly plants in the South. When one of these trains, like the appropriately named *Spark Plug*, rolls out of Cincinnati, it literally becomes a part of the production line of assembly plants in Atlanta.

Southern No. 6915, E-8 arriving in Washington early in the morning pulling Southern's crack passenger train, the *Southern Crescent* (before Amtrak). Engine No. 6915 was destroyed on May 26, 1978, after hitting a loaded lumber truck at Norcross, Ga.

— Norfolk Southern Corp.

Southern Railway's Appalachia yard at Appalachia, Va.

— Norfolk Southern Corp.

Solar accumulators, in the foreground, provide current to charge the storage batteries that provide power to the signals near the southern end of the Lake Pontchartrain trestle on Southern's line into New Orleans, La.

– Norfolk Southern Corp.

A loading tube is positioned over the trough-type hatch of a Southern Railway "Super Big John" aluminum-covered hopper car. With an empty weight of some 55,700 pounds, the huge cars can carry approximately ten tons more payload than a steel car of the same capacity.

– Courtesy of Southern Ry.

Southern Nos. 3984 and 3970, B23-7s, with GP-30 No. 2542 await a clear signal from Pomona Yard Tower to pull a 52-car train in from Winston-Salem, N.C.   *– Norfolk Southern Corp.*

Engine No. 7002 is the successful test model of the new GP-40X freight locomotive.

– Norfolk Southern Corp.

Norfolk Southern's Thoroughbred Locomotives. Here with its new paint scheme is an ex-Norfolk & Western GP-38.

– Norfolk Southern Corp.

Radio Car No. 5935 and Southern Nos. 3042 and 3078 are all part of a radio train. A radio train has 3 or 4 lead units and 2 or 3 engines in the middle. The radio car is used so that the engineer can operate the whole train from the first lead engine.

- Southern Railway.

Norfolk Southern No. 1606, DRS 6-6-15. This Baldwin-built engine works the yard in Raleigh, N.C., in 1972. Note that the gondolas have orange ends. These cars are for Maintenance of Way Service only.

- Norfolk Southern Corp.

Coal transloader and a coal unit train. Here the transloader is fed from the mines and then loads coal cars when a unit train arrives.

— *Southern Railway.*

Southern Railway's "Big Red" hopper car, built for unit train service, is able to carry up to 106 tons of coal. The car is equipped with air-controlled hatches which permit it to be unloaded as the train passes over the unloading station at a power plant at three to four miles per hour.

— *Southern Railway*

Another award-winning idea came in 1983, when Southern converted 50-foot boxcars into 50-foot flatcars to haul the new 45- and 48-foot trailers. The conventional 89-foot flatcars were designed to handle two of the standard 40-foot trailers, but they could not handle the new extra-length trailers. Southern had on hand a fleet of surplus 50-foot boxcars, and three prototype units were developed from these cars, one at Southern's Coster Shop in Knoxville. The top part of the car was removed down to the floor, then with some modifications, an adjustable trailer hitch was installed. The new cars can handle trailers up to 50 feet in length. The first cars were put into service in September 1983, and by the end of that year 170 more cars were in service throughout the system.

Another of Southern's innovations is the unit train. It is vital that huge quantities of coal move quickly and reliably from the mines to power plants at a low cost. The unit train was introduced in the United States by Southern more than 20 years ago, and it has proved to be the answer for more and more utility companies and railroads. A unit train shuttles back and forth between one origin and one destination with no expensive and time-consuming switching or car interchange en route.

Movement is the name of the game in transportation, and the unit trains are almost always on the move. One of the unit trains regularly makes a 900-mile round trip between coal mine and power plant in about 55 hours. Each of the trains hauls, on the average, more than a million tons of coal a year.

If you are beginning to get the impression from all this that Southern looks on transportation as a service to be turned out to the customer's specifications, you're right. Transportation *is* a service, and it is more perishable than any product. There's no stockpiling here.

Consider, if you will, the complications of producing something that is constantly being assembled, taken apart and put back together again in a new form. This is the challenge a railroad faces 24 hours a day, 365 days a year. One of the settings in which this happens is a freight classification yard, where cars are classified according to their destinations. But the control these days is more and more electronic.

Closed-circuit television scans the trains entering the yard, and the sequence of cars in the train is recorded, leading to the automatic switching of each car onto the proper track. Radar detects each car's speed as it rolls down the incline, with a computer determining the speed required for a gentle coupling and automatically signaling the retarders just how much to slow the car down. In olden days, all this had to be done by hand and by groundmen.

As cars move through yards and terminals, information about their movement, contents and destinations is electronically transmitted to Atlanta, and there it is fed into a computer memory. Up-to-the-minute information on the movement of every car on Southern's lines is instantly available to the company and its customers.

With their yard at Linwood, N.C., Southern now operates eight of these electronic classification yards. Each one can move thousands of freight cars a day. (And they think of these yards in terms of how many cars they can move, not how many cars they can hold.)

Modern manufacturing methods play a vital part in many other railroad operations as well. Locomotive maintenance, for example, has long since outgrown the roundhouse. When a diesel unit completes its 30-day tour of duty, its last stop is a centralized repair shop at Atlanta or Chattanooga. The shop is like an industrial production line. Each locomotive moves through various shop points, where it is cleaned, tested, lubricated, equipped with any new parts needed and given any other servicing required.

Even track-laying, once dependent on the gandy dancers' muscle power, has undergone a vast change because of mechanization. Today, track is laid with quarter-mile-long welded ribbons of steel rather than short rail sections. It is carried to the job site on special rail trains that can hold 15 miles of ribbon rail, enough for 7½ miles of track. Here specially designed equipment helps Southern renew its steel lifeline with greater speed and economy.

People who have the chance to look behind the scenes at Southern Railway are often surprised to find so much modern technology at work within one of the nation's oldest industries. As it happens, railroads are among the most receptive of all businesses to technological advances. Two related areas, communications and computers, help underline this point.

Southern operates one of the largest private microwave systems in the country. This network makes it possible for anyone on the railway to be in person-to-person contact with anyone else anywhere on the System. It also opens the way for numerous other benefits of rapid communication.

Centralized Traffic Control (CTC) enables a dispatcher at a central location to direct train movement on hundreds of miles of track. This allows their tracks to carry more traffic at higher speeds with greater safety.

Spencer Yard at Linwood, N.C. as well as the classification tracks, the yard has sanding, refueling, repair and cleaning areas. Photo was taken in 1979.

- Norfolk Southern Corp.

Night scene at Linwood Yard. With the bright lights, the yardmaster can see a very long way. — *Norfolk Southern Corp.*

Southern's communications network channels information constantly to the railway's operations nerve center, the control and coordination center in Atlanta. Here you'll find officers from every department of the railway dealing with the 24-hour-a-day job of keeping freight moving on 9,966 miles of railroad. The General Superintendent of Transportation is on duty here, the man on the spot for hundreds of critical operating decisions, making sure that the unit coal trains, the auto parts trains and all the other "must" trains will be where they are needed and on time.

Southern has been involved with computers since the early days of data-processing. Now into the fifth generation of computer hardware, they have built up such a treasure trove of computer-based information and programming that they can put all sorts of interesting questions to the computers. And get answers. How high or wide a load can be sent along a given route? What precautions need to be taken? If the load is too big to move that way, what's the alternate route? Suppose a train schedule is changed, how will it affect operations elsewhere on the System? How soon will another classification yard be needed? What's the best location for it? Where is car number 8074?

Many of Southern's customers are equipped to make direct contact with the railroad's computer via telephone or telegraph systems for a direct printout of information on the location and movement of one or a fleet of their cars.

Southern relies on advances in technology, in computers and in every other field, but they never lose sight of the fact that people are their most important resource. Southern known that any company that is not actively in the business of developing its human resources may not be in business for long. That's why personnel development is a way of life on the Southern Railway. They put a premium on performance and believe that it is a product of ability, motivation and training. They consciously seek out people who measure their own careers in terms of performance, and then give them the best training possible.

Training and experience help Southern Railway employees do a better transportation job now, but they are also in preparation for the future.

What kind of future will it be? Some things are pretty clear in an otherwise clouded crystal ball. It will be a time of challenge and change, and of increasing demand for transportation.

Transportation is vital to a mass-distribution economy, and will be for as far ahead as anyone can see. Many and varied carriers take part in it, but the indispensable base is a healthy and vigorous railroad industry. Not just a few solvent railroads, but a strong railroad industry. When you think about the future in terms of our hard-pressed natural resources and our threatened environment, another fact about railroads is worth remembering. Out of all the forms of mass transportation, railroads make the least demands on our energy resources, and they have the least polluting effect on our environment.

The strength of all railroads and how well they can work together is important to the Southern. Computer-to-computer interchange of information by railroads, as they now interchange freight cars, will help all railroads work more closely together for the benefit of customers and the public.

Locomotive engineers and signals
and communications workers
study the railroad's block signal
system on a model track set-up.
— *Norfolk Southern Corp.*

Training center at
McDonough, Ga.,
nicknamed a "rail-
road university."
The center is near
Atlanta.
— *Norfolk Southern Corp.*

At Sevier Yard, Knoxville, Tenn., work continues into the dusk as powerful lights provide illumination in the
work areas.
— *Norfolk Southern Corp.*

Another advance in inter-railroad cooperation is the run-through train. Such trains operate over two or more railroads, using locomotives from all the railroads involved. The train gets the green light all the way, bypassing intermediate yards and avoiding the interchange of cars between railroads at terminal points. This cuts transit time and greatly increases the reliability of long-distance freight service.

But run-through trains are only a step in the direction of a more fundamental change in the nation's thinking about transportation. Long-range requirements are for a unified approach to the transportation needs of the country. Looking to the future, more and more people are beginning to think in terms of total surface transportation companies, rather than carriers limited to a single mode of transportation. The logic of total transportation is compelling. It is a concept that puts the focus on the goal instead of the means of getting it there.

Southern operates a rapidly growing inter-modal service combining the best features of both rail and highway transportation, having a large fleet of trailers and containers, and hundreds of flatcars to carry them, as well as approximately 40 transfer points where the exchange between road and rail can be made.

It's a long way from the *Best Friend of Charleston*. But in another sense, Southern is coming full circle. The predecessor company of Southern that put this little steam locomotive into regularly scheduled service and helped launch this country's railroad industry called itself The South Carolina Canal & Rail Road Company. They were thinking total transportation a century and a half ago.

In 1968, Mr. W.S. Geeslin had the idea for an Exhibit Car. Southern's Exhibit Car is a gathering of modern displays in a showcase on wheels. Mr. A.S. Eggerton got the job of seeing a Pullman car converted into such a showcase. Mr. Eggerton explained that "the company wanted a link between itself and the communities it serves. An Exhibit Car, telling the story of a modern and progressive Southern Railway through various exhibits, seemed an excellent tool."

Working with personnel at Southern's Hayne Car Shop, Spartanburg, S.C., and a Washington, D.C., design firm, Mr. Eggerton helped create the Exhibit Car in 12 months. In 1977, the Exhibit Car went through a major overhaul. It was repainted, both inside and out, and a diesel generator was added to give it its own electrical system. Previously, a power car supplied energy.

In 1983, after another major overhaul and many months of planning, redesigning and building, the new Exhibit Car made its premiere showing at July 4th activities in Quincy, Ill., as the Norfolk Southern Exhibit Car, sporting the corporate colors and logo. Visitors' introduction to the car is a brief glance at railroad history. The birth and growth of railroads, and the Southern in particular, are chronicled in colorful words and pictures; a tale of rails, sails, live horses and iron horses, steam and diesel. But the real story in the Exhibit Car is the exciting, intricate saga of advancing railroad technology in the computer age, and how Southern harnesses scientific advancements to transportation challenges.

The Exhibit Car presents a new concept of the shape of railroading in these exciting times. Its presentation of how the Southern serves through transportation technology highlights:

– A system-wide microwave communications network — one of the largest in the world for private industry.
– Computers — fifth-generation hardware which can help control operations and keep to management supplied with up-to-the-minute information required for effective decision-making.
– Centralized Traffic Control (CTC) — enabling one man to control train movements on hundreds of miles of track, assuring train safety and efficient movement with the flick of a switch.
– Automated, computerized classification yards, where each car entering is promptly but gently sorted into the first available train toward its destination.
– Cars designed to carry special cargo — coal, automobiles, leaf tobacco, grain, lumber, pulpwood, woodchips — with economy and efficiency.
– Run-through trains which operate on two or more railroads without classifying or changing motive power, and unit trains which speed a single commodity.
– Hot-box detectors — trackside devices that alert operating personnel to overheated wheel bearings.
– Mobile agents, each covering several towns in a radio-equipped vehicle from a single base station.
– Welded ribbon rail that takes the "clickety-clack" and the wear and tear out of the rails.
– Piggybacking, the intermodal concept that combines speed and dependability with door-to-door delivery.

A view inside the Exhibit Car. — *Norfolk Southern Corp.*

Southern's Exhibit Car tours the system with displays and exhibits which illustrate how a modern railroad works.
— *Norfolk Southern Corp.*

New Orleans intermodal facility simplifies trailer/container handling. A giant overhead gantry crane, rail mounted and movable, prepares to lift a trailer from the train.

– Norfolk Southern Corp.

This Southern Railway all-door 90-ton boxcar, is from a prototype designed by the railway.

– Norfolk Southern Corp.

Before all the cars are loaded, this 97-car unit train will nearly meet itself coming the other way.

- *Norfolk Southern Corp.*

The Southern Companies' coal transloader on the Tennessee River at Pride, Ala. in 1975.

- *Norfolk Southern Corp.*

Southern put solar panels atop some 80 cabooses to provide power to the rear-end lighting.
— *Norfolk Southern Corp.*

The "Go Team" displays some of the equipment it will use in responding to train accidents involving hazardous materials.
— *Norfolk Southern Corp.*

Humping cars by computer. A highly automated classification hump yard at Sheffield, Ala.

- Norfolk Southern Corp.

Southern is still thinking that way. And, in spite of all the changes that have revolutionized railroading over the years, they are still seeking the goal of the railroad pioneers, to make transportation meet the needs of the people.

Some of the railroads that make up the Southern Railway are:

Alabama Great Southern
Atlantic & East Carolina
Carolina & Northwestern
Central of Georgia
Interstate
Live Oak, Perry & South Georgia
Louisiana Southern
New Orleans & Northwestern
Cincinnati, New Orleans & Texas Pacific
Georgia & Florida
Georgia Northern
Georgia, Southern & Florida
New Orleans Terminal
Norfolk Southern (the old one)
Savannah & Atlanta
State University Railroad
Tennessee, Alabama & Georgia
Tennessee Railway
Tennessee Central   "LOOK AHEAD — LOOK SOUTH"
Mobile & Ohio   SOUTHERN RAILWAY
Blue Ridge
Tallulah Falls
and many, many more.

On June 1, 1982, a "new" railway system came into being. Its name is the Norfolk Southern Corporation, the result of the merger of the Southern Railway and the Norfolk & Western. Consolidation of Southern and Norfolk & Western united two of the nation's most efficient railroads. The new system serves a territory of 20 states and operates a rail network of about 18,000 miles, making it the fourth largest railroad in terms of road mileage in America.

As a result of the merger, Norfolk & Western now has car shops at Roanoke, Va., which can construct open-top hoppers, covered hoppers and open gondolas at costs that are substantially less than an outside supplier. Thus, the Norfolk & Western can build more cars, for both railroads, more efficiently, enabling them to minimize costs, which will ultimately benefit shippers. And Southern has a rail-welding plant in Atlanta which has the capacity to produce continuous welded "ribbon" rail for both railroads.

The railroads expect that there will be better utilization of the existing car fleets, minimizing additional equipment needs. The freight will move faster, cost will be lower, and railroad cars will spend less time in transit. There will also be an annual savings of 5 million gallons of diesel fuel.

With the merger, there are five new principal routes: (1) The Altavista Gateway — Portsmouth, Ohio — Roanoke, Va. — Altavista, Va. — Spencer Yard at Linwood, N.C., (2) The Lynchburg — Knoxville Cutoff — Potomac Yard at Alexandria, Va. — Lynchburg, Va. — Bristol, Va./Tenn. — Knoxville, Tenn., (3) The Mid-South Corridor — Chicago — Cincinnati — Atlanta; Detroit — Cincinnati — Atlanta; and Bellevue, Ohio — Cincinnati — Atlanta; (4) The Kansas City Gateway — Kansas City, Mo. — St. Louis, Mo. — Louisville, Ky.; and Kansas City, Mo. — Moberly, Mo. — Decatur, Ill. — Altavista, Va. — Spencer Yard; (5) The Shenandoah Corridor — Hagerstown, Md. — Lynchburg, Va. — Spencer Yard, and Hagerstown, Md. — Bristol, Va./Tenn. — Knoxville, Tenn.

With the consolidation, there is still a Southern Railway and a Norfolk & Western Railway. They are still the same strong, well-managed railroads, but now they operate as a team, with a single goal, a single purpose and a single direction.

Southern serves the South today, just as it has in the past and will in the future.

Quarter-mile ribbons of rail are fed from a quarter-mile long train for laying track on Norfolk Southern's Norfolk line. This project is on the five mile long Norfolk Southern trestle across Albermarle Sound between Mackeys and Edenton, N.C.

– *Norfolk Southern Corp.*

Quarter-mile lengths of welded rail are made continuous by welding the ends together while the track is in place. Here a weld is formed with molten metal heated in the crucible at the left in a thermite process.

– *Norfolk Southern Corp.*

149

In 1969, then Southern President W. Graham Claytor, Jr. asked Mr. William J. Purdie, Jr. to start rebuilding steam engines for excursion use. Since that time Mr. Purdie has supervised the restoration of eight locomotives: No. 750, a 4-6-2 Pacific type; No. 630, a 2-8-0 Consolidation type; No. 722, a 2-8-0 Consolidation type; No. 4501, a 2-8-2 Mikado; No. 610, a 2-10-4 Texas type; No. 2839, a 4-6-4 Royal Hudson Class; No. 2716, a 2-8-4 "Kanawha" type; and No. 611, a NW "J" Class. Mr. Purdie has logged about 200,000 miles on them as troubleshooter and engineer. He has said, "They're like living, breathing things when they get fired up and working. I've gotten to where I almost feel kin to them."

Southern's steam excursion program started in a substantial fashion in 1968 and has been growing every since. More than 600,000 passengers have ridden these excursions and countless hundreds of thousands have witnessed the wonderful spectacle from trackside. The steam program preserves Southern's steam heritage and provides miles and miles of recreation for the general public in the territory that Southern serves.

The Southern Railway has operated steam locomotives 630, 722, 750, 4501, and also the Norfolk & Western engine No. 611. Southern leased two other engines, Nos. 610 and 2839, but they have been returned to their owners. Engine No. 2839 is an ex-Canadian Pacific Railway locomotive and was of the Royal Hudson Class (4-6-4). Her working life was spent running between Toronto and Fort William, Ont., and she pulled such trains as the *Dominion*. On November 30, 1980, No. 2839 ran extra north on her way back to her owners, for use on the Wilmington & Western Railroad in Delaware. The last report on her said that she was doing yard work on the Wilmington & Western.

Engine No. 610, of the 2-10-4 Texas type, took its name from the Texas & Pacific Railway. It was used in heavy freight service. No. 610 was of the first ten of this type built in 1927. No. 610 was returned to Fort Worth, Texas, in January 1981, where she was to be put on display.

Steam locomotive 630 was obtained by Southern in 1967. She was one of two venerable steam engines received from the East Tennessee & Western North Carolina Railroad Company in exchange for two Southern Railway ALCO diesels. The other engine was 722. Essentially, the two steam engines were returning home, as they originally belonged to Southern and had been sold to the ET&WNC shortly before Southern completed its shift to diesel power in 1953. Southern wanted the two locomotives back for display and excursion purposes. Engine No. 630 was built in Richmond, Va., in 1903, and is of the 2-8-0 Consolidation type. The first scheduled run of engine 630, after it was reacquired, was made on February 24, 1968, when it pulled a train of railfans out of Birmingham on a three-day trip. Steam engine 722 was Baldwin-built in 1904, also a 2-8-0 Consolidation type. After the extensive restoration work required to bring it up to Southern's "steam" standards, 722 made its debut on September 4, 1970, by pulling a trainload of railfans from Augusta, Ga., to Charleston, S.C.

Savannah & Atlantic locomotive No. 750 is of the Pacific 4-6-2 type. She was built in January 1910 by the American Locomotive Company (ALCO) in Schenectady, N.Y., for the Florida East Coast Railway. In 1932 she was set aside and was sold to the Savannah & Atlantic in October 1935. The locomotive became No. 750 on the S&A, and for approximately 15 years she hauled both passenger and freight trains. After the S&A was dieselized, 750 was the only steam engine retained for standby service. On July 4, 1962, the Savannah & Atlantic Railway donated No. 750 to the Atlanta Chapter of the National Railway Historical Society for exhibition and excursion operations. This engine has powered numerous excursion trains since that time.

Locomotive No. 4501 is of the Mikado 2-8-2 type and is the property of the Tennessee Valley Railroad Museum in Chattanooga, Tenn. She was built for the Southern Railway by the Baldwin Locomotive Works in 1911. Some say that she was the first "Mike" under steam in the Southland, but at any rate she spurred a whole breed of Mikados. Southern eventually acquired over 400 Mikados. In 1948 she was in a scrap line at Princeton, Ind., when she was noticed by officials of the Kentucky & Tennessee Railway. They purchased her, gave her the number 12, and assigned her to haul coal trains between Stearns, Ky., and the coal tipples not too far away. Toward the end of 1963, the K&T switched to diesels, and for a second time K&T's No. 12 was out of a job. The following year, the Tennessee Valley Railroad Museum became a Valhalla for her and she regained her maiden number, 4501. She is now dressed the green-and-gold livery that made Southern passenger steam power so popular, and she rests in the company of the TVRM's growing collection of rail relics.

Norfolk & Western's No. 611 was one of the 14 4-8-4 Northerns of the "J" class built in May 1950 in the Norfolk & Western's Roanoke, Va., shops. When steam passenger service came to an end on October 24, 1959, 611 became the property of the Roanoke Transportation Museum, where she remained on open display for some 20 years. Norfolk & Western used the "J's" to power the *Powhatan Arrow, Pocahantas* and *Cavalier* in mainline service between Cincinnati and Norfolk, Va.

In October 1981, Mr. Robert B. Claytor, Norfolk Southern chairman, announced that 611 would be restored to operating condition as a gift from the Norfolk & Western to the people of Roanoke for the city's 1982 centennial celebration. No. 611 was towed to Southern Railway's Norris Yard steam shop at Birmingham, where she came under the experienced hands of Master Mechanic William J. Purdie. On August 14, 1982, the most exciting moment of the restoration came when 611 moved under her own power for the first time since her retirement. On August 22, 1982, 611 had a homecoming back in Roanoke, Va., when she pulled in on track four under her own steam. The mighty "J" was home.

Engine Number 2716 is an ex-Chesapeake & Ohio 2-8-4, a "Kanawha"-type steam locomotive. She was built by the American Locomotive Company (ALCO) in 1943 and ran in both freight and passenger service until the mid-1950s. She appeared on the Southern for the 1981-82 excursion season.

Southern No. 4501. She was built in 1911 by Baldwin. No. 4501 is now the property of the Tennessee Valley Railroad Museum.

- Norfolk Southern Corp.

Here No. 4501 passes
a lake.

- Norfolk Southern Corp.

Southern No. 4501 with a full train of cars rolls through the southern countryside.   *- Norfolk Southern Corp.*

Savannah & Atlanta No. 750, 4-6-2. She was built in 1910 by ALCO in Schenectady, N.Y., for the Florida East Coast Ry. Here she makes excursion run in Georgia, 1967.

- Norfolk Southern Corp.

Here are engines 722 and 750 as they doublehead this excursion train. The rail fan had a real treat on this run.

– Norfolk Southern Corp.

154

Engine 630 makes an excursion run through Georgia.

- Norfolk Southern Corp.

With a full head of steam and a full train, 630 makes the grade.

- Norfolk Southern Corp.

Smoke billows from engine 630 as she pulls an excursion train. Engine 630 is of the 2-8-0 Consolidation type.

- Norfolk Southern Corp.

Ex-Canadian Pacific No. 2839, 4-6-4. She was built in 1937. Here she pulls into Monroe, Va., in 1979, on her way to Birmingham, Ala.
- Norfolk Southern Corp.

Here Southern marking may be seen clearly. Note that the beaver logo of the Canadian Pacific has been replaced. Workmen connect water lines while two rail fans look on. Photo was made in 1980 in Danville, Va.
- Author's collection.

Ex-Norfolk & Western No. 611, 4-8-4. She is of the "J" Class and the last of her kind. She still wears Norfolk & Western markings.

– Author's collection.

Southern No. 1401 Ps4 built by the Richmond, Va., works of the American Locomotive Company (ALCO) in 1926. She is now on display at the Museum of American History, Smithsonian Institute, in Washington, D.C.

– Norfolk Southern Corp.

Ex-Texas & Pacific No. 610. She was built in 1927 and is of the Texas type 2-10-4. She was leased by Southern for excursion operations in the late 1970s. Photo was taken in Danville, Va., 1978. — *Author's collection.*

Southern (GS&F) No. 8344 westbound at Constitution, Ga., on local freight, 1951.
- *Photo by R.D. Sharpless, collection of Frank E. Ardrey, Jr.*

Credits

The South Carolina Group, The Virginia Group, The Tennessee River Group. - *History of the Southern Railway.*

Central of Georgia Railway. - *History of the Central of Georgia.*

The Alabama Great Southern. - *History of the Alabama Great Southern.*

The Charlotte and South Carolina Railroad. - *History of the Southern Railway.*

The Marriage of the Waters. - *Ties Magazine, 1953, Page 12-14.*

Macon and Brunswick. - *History of the Macon and Brunswick.*

The Confederacy Mounts its Iron Horse. - *Ties Magazine, April 1961, pages 16-17.*

Big Battle at Manassas - *Ties Magazine, August 1961, pages 6-8.*

Rails Across A Battleground. - *Ties Magazine, December 1958, pages 10-15.*

When Artillery First "Took to the Rails". - *Ties Magazine, December 1961, pages 10-11.*

The Piedmont Railroad. - *Ties Magazine, February 1965, pages 9-11.*

Portrait in Power Smoke. - *Ties Magazine.*

Last Days of the "Lost Cause". - *Ties Magazine.*

Callaway's Cold War with the Union Army. - *Ties Magazine, June 1959, pages 11-13.*

The Cincinnati-New Orleans Line. - *History of the Cincinnati-New Orleans.*

Frontier Surgeon. - *Ties Magazine.*

A Scholar on the High Iron. - *Ties Magazine.*

Cincinnati Southern Railway. - *History of the Cincinnati Southern.*

Tiger in the Saddle. - *Ties Magazine.*

Louisville Southern Railroad. - *History of the Louisville Southern.*

Cincinnati, New Orleans and Texas Pacific. - *History of the Cincinnati, New Orleans and Texas Pacific Railroad.*

Norfolk Southern Railway. - *History of the Norfolk Southern Railway.*

Southern Railway System. - *History of the Southern Railway.*

Central of Georgia Railway. - *History of the Central of Georgia Railway.*

Wreck of Old 97. - *Railroad files, Danville Register, September 28 to October 2, 1903, and personal investigation.*

Death of Samuel Spencer. - *Danville Register, November 29, 1906.*

Fire at Danville Station. - *Danville Register, January 31, 1922.*

The Southern Crescent. - *A History of Good Service.*

Wreck of Number 52. - *Danville Register, May 3, 1933.*

FDR's Funeral Train. - *Southern Railway files.*

Milepost 10,000 plus. - *Ties Magazine, 1963.*

The "Go Team". - *Southern Railway files.*

"Mobile Agent". - *Southern Railway files.*

Sheffield Yard. - *Southern Railway files.*

Southern Railway: Takes Pride in Transloader. - *Ties Magazine.*

The Southern Crescent, End of an Era. - *Press Release, March 2, 1978.*

Spencer Yard. - *Ties Magazine.*

Southern Railway's Exhibit Car. - *Southern Railway files.*

What Does A Railroad Mean to You. - *Story of the Southern Railway.*

NW-Southern Merger. - *Press Release.*

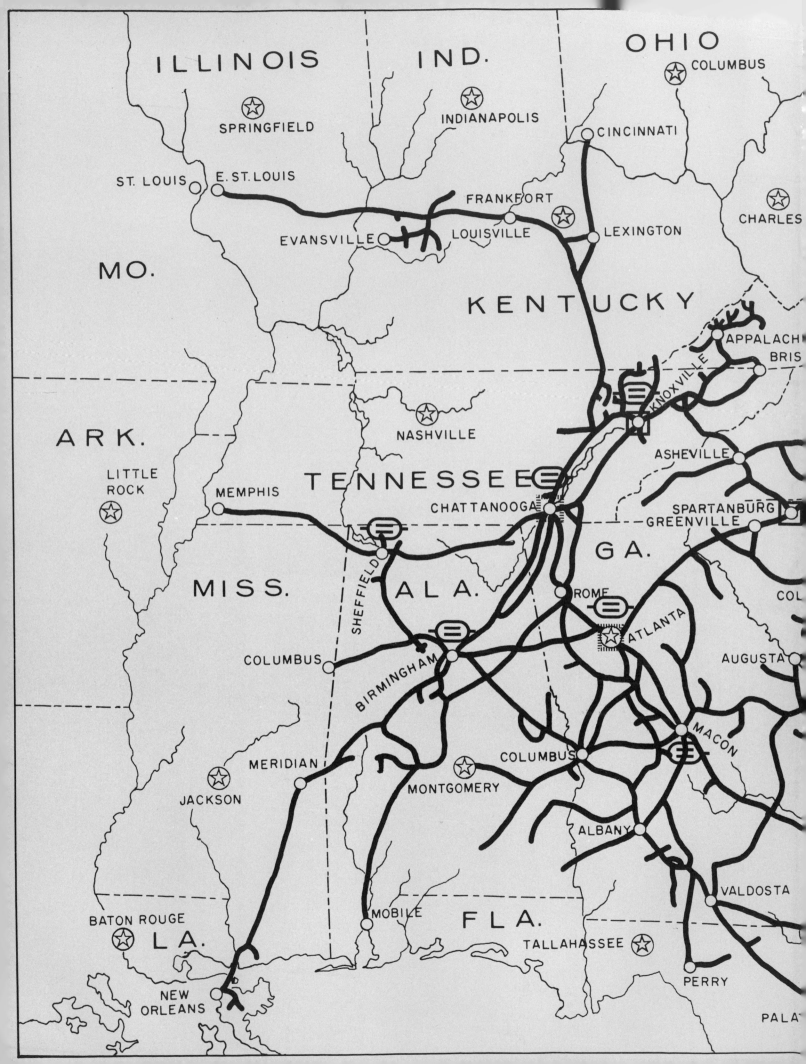